"Ross Lovelock's major gift lies in his obses... humour, a reliance on hard facts and a quick impatience for rhetoric, have over and again proved invaluable in helping organizations correctly pinpoint and address their toughest challenges."

David W. Henderson , Chief Talent Officer and SVP, Human Resources MetLife

"Ross Lovelock, an incredible creative and passionate CEO with huge intellectual capacity who knows the real business world inside out and who delivers the SCQuARE content in such an entertaining and powerful way that you can't step away from training without being infected by the SCQuARE way of thinking."

Ulf Werkmeister, Vice President, Human Resources, Unilever DACH

"Ross is an acquired taste. I've been happy to acquire him to work on a number of important business challenges over the last decade. Like a fine wine, uncork him, let him and the team breathe and enjoy the taste of a completed plan and empowered team."

Vince Robinson, President, Nestle Walmart, USA

"SCQuARE enabled our organization to reduce the time dedicated to developing our annual strategic plan from 6 weeks to 6 days. Moreover, the SCQuARE Framework ensures that all strategies are spelt out in absolute terms so that we constantly deliver on time and budget while delivering the business growth required."

Lindsay Kelly, Managing Director, EXIMO, Australia

"The investment in SCQuARE repaid itself in the first 6 months. It reduced our 'Planning for Growth' cycle by over 50% . . . and that is being conservative. All of those that undertook SCQuARE were able to more rapidly identify the key problem or opportunity and address it rather than wasting time on solving the wrong problem."

Dominique Pomario, HR Manager, Recruitment & Development, Flight Centre Australia

"Quite simply, SCQuARE works. After we introduced it, incredibly 9 out of 10 targets have been won! SCQuARE has proved a great sales tool."

Rod Hyde, Head Of Consumer Finance, HSBC Australia

"I'm surprised to report that this is the single, best training of this type that I've ever attended. Many courses are useful, some are even interesting, but this one's value for the time spent is unparalleled. Thank you! We need to implement this corporate-wide."

Debra Barker, Global Head of Clinical and Medical Services, Novartis A.G.

"From my perspective, the benefits of SCQuARE for us have been threefold: improved critical thinking skills, a consistent way to frame a business case for action, and more efficient communications and decision-making."

Don DeGolyer, President, Sandoz USA

"SCQuARE enabled us to work through one of our most difficult challenges . . . The creation of a Global Brand Import model for Wal-Mart . . . this is now done and set to deliver an instant ROI."

JC Jove, VP Global Accounts, PepsiCo

"SCQuARE is a near-perfect tool for strategic planning."

Seni Adetu, Group Managing Director & CEO, East African Breweries Limited

"I think we all agree that this is a wonderful workshop for us to map out strategy for Revlon China. All of this is done collaboratively and intensively."

Edward Yu, General Manager, Revlon, China

"SCQuARE enabled us to achieve in four days what would normally take six months!"

David Teasdale, SVP & Asia Managing Director, Revlon

"I first came to experience SCQuARE back in 2008 when I was working with another organization as head of training. I was delightfully surprised that the elements of SCQuARE were quite similar to what I practised in the Army, called Combat Appreciation. SCQuARE gives me breadth and depth in looking at issues and providing the platform for me to process my thoughts to influence my stakeholders. Hence, in January 2013, I was fortunate to be able to share this experience with my new team members in PETRONAS, and was happy to note, they feel the same way too."

Noor Iskandar Hashim, Director, Advanced Leadership Development Division, PETRONAS Leadership Centre, Malaysia

"SCQuARE is the best formal training course that I have attended in my career.
It changed the way I think about problems, enabling better solutions and making the process much quicker and less painful. I wish everyone had this knowledge, so that we can save time on endless discussions . . . SCQuARE eliminates these vicious circles."

Igor Makarov, Vice President, Chief Marketing Officer, The Walt Disney Company CIS LLC, Russia

"Attending the SCQuARE programme will go down as one of the most memorable events in my career."

Rajdeep Dattagupta, Planning Director, Pepsi, India

"Ross Lovelock is a very clever and experienced consultant with whom I have worked in the past. His methods are innovative, creative and, above all, work to the benefit of his clients. Any book by Ross is as good as a book by the great Dr Eliyahn Goldratt."

Professor Malcolm McDonald, Emeritus Professor, Cranfield School of Management

"Ross is an inspirational leader of change. He truly has a unique style that engages, challenges and inspires people to be better leaders in today's complex and challenging business world."

Simon Hay, Global CEO, dunnhumby

THE ONE THING YOU NEED TO KNOW

The SCQuARE way to better business
planning and decision making

ROSS LOVELOCK

WILEY

DEDICATION

To David Jones, Peter Kendall and Wayne Mailloux

Three mentors who gave me a chance in my career when nobody

else would. Without their help and friendship I would not have

started SCQUARE and this book would not have been written.

contents

Contents

foreword

'I've got a lunchtime presentation
tomorrow and my boss says he
expects the usual tripe.
Do you have any?'

Foreword from Justin King

Chief Executive, J. Sainsbury Plc

AT the heart of most businesses are people. In competitive markets, the organisations that win are those that are best at listening to and communicating with people.

Dialogue with customers is widely recognised as critical for business success. It is generally accepted that the organisation that is not listening to its customers is doomed to failure.

Equally important is dialogue with colleagues. Listening to colleagues is central to our way of working at Sainsbury's, whether via our 'Tell Justin' suggestion scheme or via the everyday discussions and projects of our management teams.

We have found that to help these management discussions and projects to be really productive – to help our people get everyone on the same page and get to yes – our managers benefit from a common and structured approach.

We have engaged the services of SCQUARE International over a number of years and the SCQuARE process is an extremely sound approach to ensuring that ideas, strategies and plans are robustly developed.

Importantly, when the SCQuARE process is shared more widely then it helps the alignment levels within the business. But, above all, SCQuARE ensures that the really bright ideas and plans get through the corporate maze to the top and this means better business, more motivated people and greater value creation.

'Listen, I've got far too many
worries to start worrying about
worrying too much!'

Every problem has in it the seeds of its own solution. If
you don't have any problems you don't get any seeds

Norman Vincent Pearle

PREFACE

NOW that I am in my fifties, when I look back on my career I see
successes and failures and sometimes, great hopes dashed.
I look back on times of different tempos – sometimes smooth and exhilarating
and sometimes scary and worrying. But through all of these things I am reminded
that worries get resolved and problems are sorted out – it's all the normal to and
fro of all normal lives and normal people.

Even great men keep a sense of perspective. Sir Winston Churchill writing in
Their Finest Hour recalls his worries about the progress of WWII and the problems
in Europe. With his renowned wit he reminds us:

> *'When I look back on all these worries I remember the story of
> the old man who said on his deathbed that he had had a lot of
> trouble in his life, most of which had never happened.'*

and then, with true perspective, he goes on to plan for and lead the country to
what we now recall as our finest hour.

Yes, worries and problems are the 'stuff' of life and the 'stuff' of careers and work – and like the old man in the story, you will have a lot of troubles that never happen! But, there are some troubles that you should not have and these are the main inspirations which prompted me to write this book and try to capture the word and the spirit of our approach to ideas, planning and persuading others.

Why I wrote this book

I wrote this book for four main reasons. First, early in my career I learnt a simple truth, a truth that has never let me down in over 25 years – simply being right, simply being logical, simply having all the facts, is not being persuasive.

Truly, the best ideas in the world are totally useless if you can't convince others to see what you see!

It occurred to me, very early on, that there is a synergy between **ideas, plans and persuasion** that creates the possibility of sound leadership and innovation – the two cornerstones of successful business. This insight led me to develop the SCQuARE process of turning good ideas into good plans and then convincing others of the way I was thinking. I hope that this book will help you to develop this powerful synergy.

Secondly, as I progressed in my career my jobs became bigger and my responsibilities grew. I even found that my ideas became bigger and my solutions became bolder – and sometimes even very risky! Like others before me I was maturing into, hopefully, a well-rounded leader. At each step in my growth a phenomenon became more apparent. I failed when I did not pay attention to aligning everyone's expectations and goals and I succeeded when I did.

Again, it was a lesson in leadership – I can achieve only when others can also achieve and for this synergy to prosper I must invest time in all the aligning processes. Or more colloquially, I must invest time in getting everyone on the same page.

Thirdly, I became increasingly frustrated with observing some companies using very expensive management consultants to create ideas, plans and strategies for implementation by the company's managers. Why weren't these being created by the managers themselves?

At first I thought it was because the consultants were more skilled, but this was not so. Did the consultants have better access to ideas and data? No, this was not the case. Eventually, it occurred to me that the reasons were much simpler. The managers had the ideas, the skills, the confidence – they had everything that was required – except for the training to drive their ideas through the corporate maze and persuade others that their ideas and plans were good. This book is a humble attempt to make this training and critical skill more widely available.

Finally, and probably the most important, I know that there are thousands upon thousands of good young people in industry with an awful lot more to offer if they could only express their ideas better and get their ideas through the corporate maze to YES.

Every minute of every day, great ideas are lost and high potential careers are stalled just because our young people are not trained in how to create an idea, turn it into a plan and then sell the idea and plan to their bosses. Importantly, their bosses are not trained in how to recognise an excellent idea, how to know a good plan from a bad plan and how to say YES when it is fully deserved. And so the negative cycle continues.

Imagine the productivity waste and personal frustrations that result from this, the loss of competitiveness and the loss to the economy. In fact, immeasurable loss to all, just because we haven't used our imagination and made the effort to guide and train people at work in the basic philosophy and skill to create ideas, turn them into good plans and then sell these ideas and plans to their bosses – the basic skills of getting the right ideas accepted and getting everyone on the same page.

SCQuARE gives you the power to solve these problems. Across the globe thousands of talented managers from many of the world's largest and best performing companies utilise this skill everyday. It has been a privilege to help executives – from experienced CEOs to first day managers – understand how to use SCQuARE, and in doing so, watch their careers blossom. This has also allowed us the luxury of building a truly international business, for which we are very grateful.

Introducing the SCQuARE mnemonic

At this stage I would like to give you an overview of the approach I am taking in this book to address some of the important problems and frustrations that I have just described.

The core process in the book is described by the **SCQuARE** mnemonic – it stands for **S**etting, **C**onsequences, pivotal **Qu**estion, **A**nswer, **R**ecommendations and **E**vidence.

The **'S'** and the **'C'** are the analysis stages. The **setting 'S'** is the first part of the analysis, where you investigate and build up a complete view of all the important and relevant positive factors that are related to the aim of your plan. The second stage of your analysis is to identify any factors that have changed and any factors that could complicate your progress towards your aim. In particular, you need to thoroughly understand and identify the **consequences 'C'** to any changes and complications.

Following this analysis stage you then begin the synthesis stage. This starts with identifying a fundamental question – or **pivotal question 'Qu'** – around which all the analysis 'turns'. This question leads to the best **answer 'A'** to your issues. You then build your answer into more detailed **recommendations 'R'** and you then provide real and strong **evidence 'E'** for your recommendations. Finally, you create a persuasive and compelling story that brings together all your work. Both the strength of the process and the strength of the content navigate your ideas through to YES.

Who should read and use this book

As I was writing this book I had my potential readers in my mind's eye.

My primary reader and user I envisaged to be a manager, probably in their first or second job with real responsibility – full of intelligence and talent and still full of enthusiasm. I wanted to help these managers before they lost some of their natural talent in the frustrating corporate maze.

These managers could be working in any sector – from heavy engineering to consumer product retailing, from public service to legal services. They could be working for any size of organisation but most likely they would be working for large organisations and in particular very large international organisations that rely heavily upon virtual teamwork or matrix teamwork. Most certainly, they could be from any country where managerial-type work is well established.

My secondary readers were the bosses of these talented managers. They too have ideas that get lost in the maze and so on up the chain of command. I wanted to provide a little hope before any cynicism sets in. Working together could lead to wholly new directions and energies.

Finally, I wrote the book for the CEO and the leadership team. The SCQuARE process is a very effective intervention that does address all the problems of the corporate maze and many of the important issues of alignment. I know from client experience that SCQuARE makes a powerful contribution and it does improve productivity and competitiveness.

How to get the best out of this book

There are different ways of reading this book depending upon your needs. First, I need to describe the parts of the book.

Chapters two to seven are the 'heart' of the book – these are the chapters that provide you with both conceptual learning and practical skills. These chapters have a reading text, an illustrative case study and an opportunity for you to do your own project.

If you are reading and using the book to get an in-depth view and practical skill then I would recommend that you follow the book sequentially, studying the case study in depth and also doing your own project either as you go or after you have finished reading the book.

If you are reading the book to get a real insight into the process then you can follow each chapter and the case study sequentially, but don't do your own project. If you just want an overview, then chapter one explains the main principles that underpin the SCQuARE process.

In any event the reading task is quite low. Most chapters can be read and studied within one half hour.

Also, you are not alone with the book. As a service to readers I have introduced a readers' advice line. If you have any queries or need any help then please call.

The advice line number, which is open during normal UK office hours, is **+44 (0)845 0800 888**.

Acknowledgements

Writing this book and developing my international business would not have been possible without the support, faith and constructive suggestions of many senior executives who were prepared to give my ideas and my business a chance. To all, I owe a debt of gratitude.

I would like to give special thanks to Paul Adams of British American Tobacco, Peter Krogh of FilmNet and Karen Guerra of Colgate-Palmolive, all ex-PepsiCo colleagues, without whose faith in our first year of business we would probably have never got started. Don Goulding, Nick Blazquez, Seni Adetu, Gerald Mahinda and Ekwunife Okoli, five guys from Diageo who recognized that to really win you had to get everyone on the same page and turn strategy into action, which they certainly did. Kim Stratton and Luc Hermans of Novartis for letting us show them how to get the detail of 'War and Peace' into a presentation the size of a postage stamp.

Vince Robinson of Nestlé – Vince for being the world record holder for SCQuARE attendance, as well as giving us the perfect description, 'the consultant's worst nightmare'.

Keith Wishart, Nick Garland, Ulf Werkmeister, Ray Hazley, Massimo Ambrosini, Gary Booker, Leandro Berrone, David Johnston and Don DeGolyer for being bigger believers in SCQuARE than me, and taking us around the globe with numerous multi-national giants. Paul Arnold, formerly of Saatchi and Saatchi, for telling the world he had found a tool to liberate creativity. Simon Hay of dunnhumby, a true SCQuARE fan who has built a successful global business, as well as becoming a great golfing host.

Frans Hijkoop and David Henderson for recognising the value of SCQuAREing HR in many parts of the world. Mark Fairweather and Nigel Toon for quite simply making SCQuARE *the* way of working of Allied Bakeries. I wish to make a special mention of thanks to Paul Wilkinson, Sri, Sue Harrison, Terry Goodyear and Jem Turner who have been with me almost from the start and whose contributions to the intellectual development of SCQUARE International have been immense and to Tracy Rose for her input improvements and tireless editing.

Finally, an immense thank you to Justin King of Sainsbury's for being a great supporter and for his very generous words in the foreword.

Also, I would like to thank James Noon for his collaboration in the writing of this book. Eventually, we did 'get on the same page' and we did have good fun bringing it all together into book form.

Last but not least, I would like to thank my team at SCQUARE, past and present. Quite simply, without them we would have no business.

Their dedication, creativity, professionalism and willingness to tackle any task, in every corner of the globe, are the reasons why SCQUARE has so many valued clients and why the business is a success. Ultimately, they are the inspiration for this book.

WHY YOU SHOULD READ THIS BOOK

SCQUARE International under the leadership of the author Ross Lovelock have for twenty years provided many of the world's leading companies the skill of SCQuARE enabling their people to create plans that command a decision in a fraction of the time of normal working practices. This book explains how it is done – equipping you with the single most important skill necessary to reach the top of any organisation – the ability to create and sell fool-proof plans.

The fundamental skill

Since the industrial revolution, competitive advantage has been driven by having a workforce with the ability to convert a company vision into workable plans – it is quite simply the most fundamental skill for long-term prosperity. Despite the mystique that people love to associate with such a skill there are only three critical things that matter:

- Identifying the right question
- Finding the right answer

- Building a crystal clear story enabling the audience to take a decision and make progress.

It is that simple. . . .

Yet, ask any executive irrespective of experience or industry what is the bane of their business life and you will almost certainly get the reply 'Sitting in seemingly never ending meetings listening to people present tome-like documents with no end in sight where often the only outcome is to plan yet another meeting'.

BBC research in July 2011 asked 1000 people the question: 'What would you rather do than sit through a PowerPoint presentation?'

- 20% said they would prefer to visit the dentist
- 18% would rather fill out their tax return
- 24% stated they would prefer to give up sex for the day

Why are many meetings such a painful ordeal?

Unless you have worked at one of the main strategic consultancies, you almost certainly will not have been provided with the skills to create and sell strategic plans. Often this crucial activity is reduced to filling in company templates resulting in outputs so devoid of narrative and interpretation that they are meaningless.

'Complexity is the refuge for the mediocre, but "Simplicity is the ultimate sophistication"'

Leonardo Da Vinci

If you want to reach the top then read this book because as the Harvard Professor Anthony Gardner says 'The ability to tell a story is the key to leadership' but that story has to have rock solid thinking and the lessons of this book will provide you with both.

'Without SCQuARE your plans might have great answers, but almost invariably to the wrong question.'
Gary Booker GM Consumer O2 UK

'That's right Jim . . . removing the hurdles before the race definitely contributed to my success!'

CHAPTER 1

MAKING THE CRITICAL DIFFERENCE

Imagine for a moment two companies that are more or less equal – close competitors in a tough market, of a similar size and with similar resources and with talented people almost drawn from the same recruiting pool. What makes the critical difference?

Is it product innovation? Very important, but in reality over time one steals the lead and then the other steals it back. Is it leadership? Again, very important but the CEO of one company used to be the CEO of the other! Talented managers? Again, there is a healthy recruiting exchange from one company to the other.

As you go through your imaginary list of critical differences you begin to accept that there is, in fact, very little critical difference between the two companies. And of course, that is why they are close competitors that are more or less equal.

Now, imagine I ask this question – what will make the critical difference between these two companies? As you think about this question you will begin to eliminate many potential differences until you settle on one single difference – the quality of ideas and their execution.

Without doubt, ideas are good but good ideas are even better! In fact, if you ask any CEO or HR Director what makes the critical difference they are likely to answer 'great ideas' but then go on and reflect 'but where are the great ideas?' In fact, the great ideas are there but they get lost within the company and more often than not the company is at fault for this. You know how it happens – great ideas get lost in the corporate maze.

The corporate maze; a dead end for ideas

The corporate maze is not an abstract idea – it's real and a huge drain on time and effort. It makes the CEO and Directors despair.

Remember the meetings that you have attended, like that one last week. You had a really well researched sales plan designed to resolve some conflicts between your major distributors. It's a priority issue. Then a marketing manager voiced a 'fear' about customer shopping habits and the financial controller thought the gross margin 'might' be affected. You had covered all of this but to no avail.

Again, no decision. Again, no resolution between the distributors – the very people we rely on. The CEO is not aware of this issue at the moment but it won't be long before the matter is raised.

Imagine another situation. You're a progressive young manager and you come up with a really bright idea – the sort of idea that immediately gets people excited. You write a proposal and it goes to your boss. Your boss is busy – he needs to get out a strategy report by the end of the week. Eventually, you get to see him but you are met with his comment 'I'm not sure we have the time to pursue this idea but I'll put it to my boss'.

To give him his due, he did put your idea to his boss but almost as an afterthought at the end of a budget meeting. His boss mused 'haven't we tried something like that before?' In effect, the bright idea is buried within three levels of management.

Even if your bright idea survives the three-level burial ground, at the fourth it is killed by 'finance will never approve this expenditure'. And, even if it survives the fourth, at the fifth it gets the killer blow – 'the Chairman won't like this idea'.

In effect, ideas move up and around the organisation and at each stage they can suffer a sudden death – irrespective of whether the idea is good or bad. Truly, the corporate maze does not discriminate between the quality of ideas!

Of course, you and I will smile at the corporate maze – it's the reality of corporate life, but the cost of the maze is huge. It is the critical difference. If two close competitors are similar then what will make the critical difference is not just the quality of ideas but also the ability of these ideas to get through the maze.

It doesn't stop there. Good ideas getting through the maze means greater motivation – generating even more really bright ideas. It means that ideas are turned into plans and then practical actions more quickly and more efficiently – great new products coming out on time and on budget, way ahead of the competitors. Finally, when the ideas do become reality, they work because everything crucial to success has been covered.

Creating alignment; a direct correlation with success

If the corporate maze is the problem then what is the solution? Before I answer that question let me describe how I see the corporate maze.

First, a corporate maze is a place where NO is instinctive and where caution and risk-aversion are endemic. The only ideas that can survive this part of the maze are ideas that represent no threat to the status quo and ideas that cost no money. Most certainly, your ideas that are about the future, about change and about risk are likely be killed in this part of the maze.

Secondly, a corporate maze is where theft occurs – because it's populated by artful dodgers. You know the scene. You have a good idea and sit down with your boss. After quite an intense grilling you get a NO. A week later you receive an announcement about a new initiative – your idea re-packaged and re-worded by your boss, with the acknowledgement that your idea 'inspired' your boss to develop his own! How do you feel? It's not just your idea that's been stolen; it's your motivation as well.

Thirdly, a corporate maze is where self-interest lives. Your idea only survives this part of the maze if your idea serves the self-interest of the decision makers. It enhances their careers, it makes their situation easier, it brings results to them and it creates credit for them. Most certainly, an idea that brings no self-interest benefits will get a NO.

Finally, the corporate maze is where belief and vision are non-existent and where cynicism and disdain are rife. This is the part of the maze where 'it's been done before and it didn't work then' lives.

So there we have it. Deep within the organisation we have caution, risk aversion,

'Alas – poor concept, slain by smartphone text on the very eve of presentation!'

idea theft, self-interest and cynicism. If this reminds you of Shakespeare's Hamlet then you are not wrong. The corporate maze is the place of negative power-play and the place of reactionary politics. What a waste of time and corporate energy!

It is because the corporate maze is so wasteful and damaging that the progressive CEO and the leadership team are focusing upon this issue and interestingly, most of the actions are interventions of positive politics.

Increasingly, corporations are trying to intervene in the culture of the business – asking the question: is it aligned to the competitive market? They are intervening in the relationship between the business and its environment – is it aligned to the will of the general population? They are intervening in the dynamics of competition – is it aligned to the speed of customers' changing needs?

Finally, they are intervening in the very nature of the way the business generates ideas, thinks and plans without the wasteful and damaging effects of the maze – are we aligned to good sense, high productivity and high motivation? In fact, as the CEO and the leadership team make their interventions in the way the business develops ideas, thinks and plans, an important observation is made – people in organisations are just not trained to get their ideas through the corporate maze. To do this, you have to focus on and train the individual manager and align the way they think and plan.

In effect, aligning all individual managers, each sharing the same corporate vision and productive way of working but without compromising their creativity. Each a motivated and individual person of talent, but each sharing common understandings. In effect, each manager on the same page. How we achieve this is what this book is about.

Creating alignment with SCQuARE

So creating alignment – getting everyone on the same page – is about working with individual managers to create the critical mass of new ways of working and ensuring that these ways of working are not affected by the waste and damage of the corporate maze.

In the next section I will introduce you to SCQuARE, but before I do this I just want to mention a point that I am passionate about because it represents one of the reasons why I wrote this book.

In this book I will show you an exceptional skill – and if you use this skill you will become a person capable of achieving your full potential in your career. Without reservation, this is a promise I will make to you.

With few exceptions, people who use the skill report significant changes in how their boss and colleagues see them and how their company respects them. Importantly, they report significant progress in getting things done with their boss – in other words, they get their ideas through the corporate maze to YES.

I believe that progress is made in our societies and economies because individuals in our histories became innovators and leaders. They created ideas and these ideas became part of a vision of the future. And the vision was exciting because they were able to also show how it could be achieved – they had a plan that they could prove would work.

But there is something even more powerful than innovation and leadership on its own. What creates the power are not just the idea and the plan, you have to add the ability to persuade – the ability to enthuse, the ability to excite and the ability to convince others.

In my view, why we make progress is a synergetic relationship between **ideas, plans and persuasion**. Natural leaders know this relationship and they know how powerful it can be. Possibly, nobody has spoken to you about this relationship – not at university and not in your corporate training. Yes, your mentors may have talked about innovation or planning or presentations as separate subjects, but not necessarily about these three concepts as a relationship or a synergy.

Think about it. An idea without a plan is useless; a plan without an innovative idea is a waste of time and resources. And a good idea and plan go nowhere unless they persuade people about what can be achieved. Without doubt, intelligence is useless unless it is applied.

It is not the separate concepts that are important, it is the way that these concepts come together as a whole and then how they work together to create a powerful synergy. I will show you how to create this synergy.

Introducing SCQuARE

In this book I'll show you a process that will help you achieve this personal goal as well as help your company to get everyone on the same page.

The process is called SCQuARE and as you will see later in the chapter, this is a mnemonic of **'S', 'C', 'Qu', 'A'** and **'RE'** and each part of the mnemonic has a part to play in building up your plan.

Before I describe SCQuARE in detail I would like to take a light-hearted wander around doing a jigsaw puzzle and then highlight the commonsense and integrated principles that SCQuARE is built upon.

Building a jigsaw puzzle

I often think of the principles and process of SCQuARE as a jigsaw puzzle – at the

A SIMPLE TRUTH . . .

Six months into my career at PepsiCo, my boss's boss told me that the Divisional President wanted to see a strategic plan for the impulse channel and I had to prepare it. After our meeting, I was left thinking 'What is a Pepsi strategic plan?'

So, I looked at other plans and tried to copy their format. This was fine because I knew everything that needed to be known about the channel. The trouble was I didn't know what to do with all this information. So, I wrote the plan until it looked nice and fat. It was returned, 48 hours later, with a final written comment saying, 'this is not a strategic plan it's a data dump'.

Bravely, I went to see my boss's boss and said 'You're clearly not happy with what I have done – I think I know everything there is to know about the impulse channel but I don't know what to do with it. You on the other hand, being an ex-McKinsey consultant, probably do'. Then, without fully knowing the fateful risk I was taking, I said 'If you don't help me, one of three things will happen – either I'll get fired, you'll get fired, or we both get fired'. After the words had left my mouth, I froze – you don't say things like that to your boss's boss!

But he was a great natural leader. He said, 'Let's work together'. We edited and made the complex simple, and then re-structured it into a very simple story – and a great strategic plan.

Later, we delivered the plan to the Divisional President, and within six months I was promoted.

start, a jumble of confusing pieces but at the finish, a clear picture.

In fact, doing jigsaw puzzles was a very enjoyable pastime as a child – after tea on a Sunday afternoon, Mum and Dad and I would get out the then current puzzle and do a little more. At the time, little did I imagine that the jigsaw puzzle was teaching me how to think and giving me a skill that would become a foundation stone in my life.

More important – it was the time that I realised a simple truth, a truth that has never let me down in over 25 years – simply being right, being logical, and having all the facts, is not being persuasive. Truly, all the best ideas in the world are totally useless if you can't convince others to see what you see.

I also learnt another truth. The higher I progressed, the bigger my ideas and solutions were and the more important it became to ensure that I got everyone on the same page.

'FANTASTIC! It says 3–5 years on the box and I've done it in just two weeks!'

Imagine for a moment doing a jigsaw puzzle – the tulip fields. The photograph on the box lid shows fields of yellows fading into the distance and meeting a sky of blues and whites. The picture has one feature – an empty field road. Great – 10,000 difficult pieces, all either yellow, blue or white and all so frustrating to fit together. I'll do the jigsaw puzzle – an analogy that will very quickly become clear.

The first thing I would do is study the picture. If I could build the horizon, a mix of yellows, blues and whites, then I could build out again. Even before I open the box, I am clear about what I want to achieve (the aim) and I am visualising how I will go about building the picture in the most effective way (my approach).

As I continue the visualisation, I'm breaking the jigsaw into parts, like 'build the road', and completing these parts will be important progress (main tasks leading to objectives). I am even making decisions about which parts I will do first and which later (sorting out the priorities). The second thing I would do is turn out all the pieces onto the table and make certain that they are all face up and visible. Certain pieces would be very important – the corner and border pieces. These pieces define the outer limits (the scope of the plan), and this is where I would start.

Each piece has a place next to other pieces – each piece will need to be studied and placed in similar groups (the collection and grouping of data) and each piece will need to be placed and replaced many times until it fits with its partner pieces (hypotheses and data analysis). To do this, I am asking questions, 'how does this piece fit in?' and so on.

The more I test for correct positions the more familiar I become. Eventually I reach a point of familiarisation with all the pieces such that I now see how it all fits together. This is the pivot point where everything is now clear and I know what I have to do (the strategy). From this point on, all I have to do is continue to build the parts (create and implement my plan), normally by asking questions again – 'how do I do this bit of the picture?' or 'why will this bit fit in here?' and so on.

As you can see, building the jigsaw is like building a plan and it highlights certain ideas that are very important. Ideas like: working within the scope, being clear about the aim, working with groups of data, becoming familiar with these groups until their meaning is clear, reaching the pivot point where the strategy then becomes clear and then building and implementing a plan by asking questions about how and why. And within these ideas lie the principles that SCQuARE is built upon and the principles that lead to a boss saying YES and getting everyone on the same page. Let me take you through these principles.

Sharing a clear aim

All organisations create a 'big picture' of their world as they see it. It contains understandings of the political and economic environment, markets and products, customers, skills, resources and so on. This 'big picture' is, in effect, the corporate strategy and it guides the organisation through its future.

'After months of work, the presentation went really well. Unfortunately, the CEO later pointed out that our big idea was not relevant to the company's operations.'

In most decent organisations, this strategy is broken into parts – with each part of the organisation doing its bit. Each part has objectives to be achieved and progress towards these objectives is measured. If there is a variance in results, then corrective action is taken – this creates innumerable projects within the organisation. In effect, many of the projects you undertake and/or plans you create are all part of this variance-correction process, which are all part of the 'big picture' of your organisation.

There are two important points I now want to make. First, your boss has a 'big picture' in his or her mind and this is but a sub-set of the organisation's 'big picture'. If you want to get your boss to say YES, then you must roughly share the same 'big picture'. If you do not, then your ideas, plans and strategies just do not 'fit' and you'll get a NO.

Secondly, most corrective actions in an organisation are driven by three things – weaknesses, threats and opportunities. For example, the sales team have a skill weakness so training is introduced. Or credit control is not collecting monies due as quickly as they should and this is threatening the cash position. Or your major competitor has just lost an important customer and now you have an opportunity to build your business, and so on. Some of these weaknesses, threats and opportunities are in current time whereas others are in future time – being proactive about corrective action and planning before the event.

This leads to the **first principle of my approach**. If you want to get your boss to say YES then you must share the same 'big picture' as your boss and it is imperative that you share the same aim of any corrective actions you have to plan for and then implement.

Analysis leads to insight

If you mismanage your time and priorities then you will notice many consequences. The most obvious ones are rushed decision making and poor team management. A less obvious consequence, but in my view a very important one, is that you will not analyse your problems in sufficient depth and breadth, and if this is the case then you do not gain insight, which is critical to the effectiveness of your ideas, strategies and plans.

For example, when you build a plan not only do you need to be clear about the scope you must also be very clear about the aim of your plan, because the scope and the aim determine your data collection – too broad means you have data overload and too narrow means you miss important issues.

In turn, your data collection determines how you group and analyse your data. This process leads to how you understand the central matters that have to be taken into account – this is insight. Like in the jigsaw puzzle analogy, the corners and border pieces determine the scope and the more you test the positions of pieces the more familiar you become and eventually you see what has to be done – good insights lead to good strategies.

This leads to the **second principle of my approach**. If you want to get your boss to say YES then you must define scope and you must include all relevant and important data that is indicated by that scope. Then thorough analysis will lead to thorough insight and the best strategy.

Focus on consequences

I mentioned earlier that corrective actions within an organisation lead to innumerable projects and plans. The majority of these corrective actions are due to changes and/or complications. For example, your sales are down this month and this is due to a reduction in price by your main competitor, or you have to delay the launch of a product because your packaging supplier had a production problem.

Clearly, all of these changes and complications are the 'stuff' of daily working – problems arise and problems get sorted out. At the back of your mind you are trained to ask a question, 'what has caused this?' and whether by experience and/or analysis you find a cause.

Unfortunately, this is not enough. When you go looking for causes it is a mistake to accept the first cause you identify. The first cause you find is actually a 'symptom' of another deeper cause and so on. In fact you need to pursue your causal chain analysis until you find the root causes.

Furthermore, apart from the root cause, a cause is but a consequence of its cause and so on. So, when looking at a change or complication, it is not sufficient to ask one question 'what has caused this?' you must also ask 'what are the consequences of this?' because, if you don't understand the consequence, you don't understand the issues.

In effect, having foresight and being proactive (essential qualities in strategy and planning) are a direct result of seeking consequences and this leads to the

'Watch out . . . data dump coming through . . . late for presentation !!!!'

third principle of my approach. If you want to get your boss to say YES then you must focus on the consequences of the changes and/or complications. It is not sufficient to just look at causes, you must also ask 'what is the consequence of this?' and then seek the risks or the options.

Define the Pivotal Question

Let me summarise my principles so far. You must be very clear about your scope – this defines the issues that have to be addressed. In turn, this defines the aim and, in turn, this determines what information or data you need. Your data then determines the analysis and if it is thorough, then this leads to insight. During this analysis, you need also to focus on the consequences of changes and/or complications because this identifies the risks you face or options you have. What is next?

In my jigsaw puzzle analogy I talked about sorting out all the pieces into related groups and then building parts by placing and replacing pieces until a piece fitted its neighbouring piece. As I did this, I was building up familiarity with the pieces and eventually I could see the 'whole', which then led me to know what I needed to do.

Not only does thorough analysis lead to insight, it leads also to a 'simplification' of a complex situation and eventually you see the situation for what it is. Some people say that 'you have worried a problem to death' and even though there is humour here, there is also truth – every issue or matter you face or will face has, at its very heart, a question that condenses all your analysis. This is the pivotal question around which all your data spins. When you find this question, you know what you need to do.

'My problem felt like a lion let loose in a pet shop, but my pivotal question rounded it up, and rounded it down, so now it feels more like a sleepy kitten.'

This leads to the **fourth principle of my approach**. If you want to get your boss to say YES then you must continue your analysis until you have identified the pivotal question. This shows you what you have to do – the right strategy to pursue.

First sell the problem

As you will see later in this chapter (and in the book as a whole), a strong part of the SCQuARE process is a focus on persuasion.

But its focus on persuasion is not crude or obvious. It comes from defining a very clear aim and then building up a thorough analysis focused into the pivotal question and then the clarity of the answer to this question.

In truth, what the SCQuARE process does is build up the clarity of a problem through analysis and then crystallise that problem into a very focused question.

This question is so well defined that it signifies a very clear answer – this answer being the solution or the strategy.

In effect, to sell a solution you must first sell the problem! Truly, most times when your boss says NO it is partly to do with the fact that the solution has not been 'seeded' sufficiently well in the problem that your boss perceives – like not sharing the 'big picture' or the aim. If you don't share the same problem then you will not share the same solution.

This leads to the **fifth principle of my approach**. If you want to get your boss to say YES then you must meticulously sell the problem first until your boss shares the problem in the same way that you see it. When you have done this then the boss will share your solution.

'Yes, Bill, I'm absolutely certain you can't sell your problem on eBay.'

Ask how before why

There comes a point in all planning where you have to critically evaluate the details and the logic of your plan before you present it to others. To do this you exhaustively ask the fundamental questions of 'how?' and 'why?' The answers to these questions will expose any weaknesses in your plan.

Now you can present to others and convince them that the details of your plan are well thought through. Again, the questions 'how?' and 'why?' are important – almost like a conversation with your boss, who asks 'how are you going to do this?' and 'why will that work?' and so on. Don't forget, all questions need answering and a badly answered question leads to doubt and more questioning. In no time at all what you thought was a sound plan is now in pieces.

Clearly, this could be because your plan is actually useless and deserves to fail at this point. More often than not, it's because you have presented a reason for doing something before you have presented what you are going to do. As soon as you do this, any intelligent boss (or audience) will conclude what should be done for the reasons you have stated. You might call this 'jumping to conclusions' but whatever you call it, if the conclusion your boss has 'jumped to' is different to your conclusion, you will now have to change the mind of your boss!

'Why do you do . . . oh, sorry . . . I mean how do you do.'

When you present a 'why' before a 'how' you open up the possibility that your boss will draw their own conclusion before you have a chance to explain your 'what' or your 'how' – and, unfortunately it is as simple as that. The more you present reasons first, the more NOs you will get.

This leads to the **sixth principle of my approach**. If you want to get your boss to say YES then you must take care to detail your plan in such a way as to avoid unnecessary and unfortunate questions. In particular, you must present your actions, your 'what' and 'how', before your reasons, your 'why'. This reduces the chances of your boss jumping to conclusions.

Tell a powerful story

Earlier, I mentioned one of my keen beliefs. The best idea in the world is useless if you can't sell it through the system. This may be unfortunate but it is true – it's a bit like a 'law of the commercial jungle'.

There is no doubt that good ideas do sell but generally these good ideas have actually been discussed or presented in a persuasive manner such that the clarity of the good idea is matched by the clarity of good presentation and persuasion.

Persuasion is not an afterthought or something you do at the last minute before a presentation deadline. Doing this is almost a guarantee that you will get a NO. Persuasion is something that is embedded in the process of planning. If the goal is to get everyone on the same page then persuasion is always in the background of your mind as you define the scope, define the aim, conduct the analysis, and define the pivotal question that signifies your strategy and so on.

In effect, everything you do is about persuasion. Then, at the end, all you have to do is tell the powerful story that you have developed. This leads to the **seventh and final principle of my approach**. If you want to get your boss and organisation to say YES then start your persuasion early within your thinking and planning process. Then, you are just left with the exciting prospect of telling your powerful story.

Describing the SCQuARE process

The diagram overleaf shows an overview of the SCQuARE process. It is a series of connected parts starting with 'the source' and finishing with 'the story' – with the SCQuARE mnemonic making up the central part. I shall explain these parts shortly. As you go through the SCQuARE process it stimulates your thinking by asking questions and as you find answers to these questions you build up your plan.

The SCQuARE mnemonic

THE SOURCE

RECOGNISING THE ISSUE
RELEVANT AND IMPORTANT DATA

THE START POINT AND SETTING

THE ENTITY
THE AIM
POSITIVE CONTEXT
SO WHAT?

THE CONSEQUENCES

CHANGES
COMPLICATIONS
CAUSAL CHAIN ANALYSIS
CONSEQUENCES

THE PIVOTAL QUESTION

THE MAIN ACTION
OVERCOMING CHANGES/COMPLICATIONS
EXPLOITING OPPORTUNITIES
ACHIEVING THE AIM

THE ANSWER

THE MAIN BENEFIT
STRATEGIES FOR EVALUATION

THE ACTION PLAN

MAIN IDEAS AND SUPPORT IDEAS
RECOMMENDATIONS AND EVIDENCE
RESOURCE CONTEXT
PRE-EMPTIVE QUESTIONS

THE STORY

BUILDING THE STORY BOARD
COMPELLING HEADLINES

The source; where to go looking for data

The source has two main sections – recognising the issue and selecting the relevant and important data.

Recognising the issue and selecting relevant and important data are generally straightforward. I mentioned earlier in this chapter that any corrective actions you need to take are mainly from three sources – weaknesses, threats and opportunities. In one way or another, these are highlighted by your performance against your job objectives and your job accountabilities.

More specifically, you will continually have a multitude of questions in your mind – 'what has changed?', 'what has caused this change?', 'what competitive action now requires a response?' and so on. Any one of these questions can become the issue that you now have to address.

'Now Simpkins, I had this snappy little idea in the bath this morning, and I'd just like YOU to quickly flesh it out into a highly effective five year corporate plan.'

Once an issue is recognised, then this defines the source and type of data that you will need – most of this information and data will be self-evident. However, some may not be. This latter data will become identified once you have defined the aim of the plan that will address the issue.

The Setting; establishing the basis of the plan

The setting is the first analysis stage of the SCQuARE process. It has four important sections.

First, it defines the entity – subject, scope and time frame of the issue that you are going to address. Secondly, it defines the aim you are seeking. Defining this aim is one of the most important tasks in the SCQuARE process – virtually everything you will reflect upon as you go through your planning will be directly conditioned by your aim. Remember the sage advice: if you do not know where you are going then any road will take you there!

Thirdly, you must find all the relevant and important data that creates a contextual setting – it being made up of factors such as strengths, successes and resources that help deliver the aim.

Finally, as you go through your analysis you will become familiar with it by distilling the data into key groups. These groups are subjected to the question 'so what?' until you are able to understand the positive interpretation of these factors in relation to delivering the aim.

The Consequences; the call to action

Whereas the setting creates the positive context of the issue, the consequences section looks specifically at what has changed. Generally, it is these changes that have created the issue that you are now addressing – the problem you now have to solve or the matter you now have to capitalise upon. In addition to changes, you need to look at any complications that have arisen because these will affect any plans you contemplate.

Importantly, you will thoroughly analyse all the causes that have created the change, down to the root causes, and all of the consequences of this change up to the risks and strategic options that you have. To do this you will use an analysis technique known as 'causal chain analysis'.

The Pivotal Question and Answer; problem defined, solution sold

All of your analysis of the setting and the consequences leads to defining the central question – the pivotal question, around which all your data and analysis turns. You need to think of the analysis as 'honing' into groups of factors that become clearer and clearer as the analysis progresses.

Eventually, everything you have learnt so far can be summarised into a single question and this question directs you to an answer.

The pivotal question signifies the main action that you need to take to address the issue. To do this it guides you to ask 'what is the main action I need to take to overcome my constraints and exploit my opportunities in order to achieve my aim?'

Systematically and thoughtfully refining this question and making it practical is an important task in the SCQuARE process. It leads naturally to an answer, which is the strategy, and then this leads to the action plan.

The action plan – Recommendations and Evidence; the road to execution

The action plan comprises the recommendations that you are proposing and any evidence that backs up your recommendations. These recommendations and evidence represent the 'RE' in the mnemonic.

Building the action plan is a process of asking 'how?' and 'why?' The pivotal question leads to an answer and this answer represents the strategy you will pursue. You then ask 'how will I do this?' and 'why will I do this?' (and similar questions) and from this process you identify ideas and these ideas are put into the plan. Finally, your plan is checked by asking and then answering various pre-emptive questions. These questions are the potentially difficult challenges that could arise when you are presenting your plan and seeking a decision.

The Story; creating a compelling narrative

Finally, the whole of the process is brought together into the story – in effect, the analysis, the pivotal question, the answer and your recommendations and evidence. This story is very powerful because it is designed to sell the problem first and then the solution. It is also designed to get everyone on the same page – and get good ideas through the corporate maze.

'I had hoped that the conference venue might have illustrated the pitfalls of building a plan on an ill-prepared Setting.'

*Definitiveness of purpose is the starting point of all
achievement*
W. Clement Stone

CHAPTER 2

STARTING WITH THE SETTING

In the last chapter I explained the process and mnemonic of SCQuARE. You will recall that after you have recognised an issue and selected relevant and important data you start your analysis by creating a thorough understanding of the setting or the '**S**' in the mnemonic.

Simply stated, the setting is a description of who you are, what you are looking at, where you are now and where you want to be in the future. More broadly, the setting fully describes a number of important elements and I'll look at each of these in turn.

Defining the entity; aligning around key parameters

The very first thing you do when you are using SCQuARE is to understand and define the subject, the scope and the time frame of your plan. These three elements in combination are called the 'entity'.

The subject is a definition of what you will investigate and the scope is the boundary of your investigation. The time frame is generally a period of time and/or the start and end point of your plan.

For example, if I were to investigate the new vehicle market for low-cost vehicles under two litres in Europe over the next two years then the subject is 'new vehicle market' and the scope is 'low cost vehicles under two litres in Europe' and the time frame is two years (say) 2014 to 2019.

Why am I insistent on saying that defining the entity is the very first thing you do when using SCQuARE? Well, the answer is clear – by defining the subject, and in particular the scope, you will focus on what is relevant and what is important.

In effect, the entity dictates the breadth of analysis and breadth of your strategies. This gives greater focus and stops you wasting time on irrelevancies and low priorities.

YOUR EXERCISE

Think of a real project that you will have to undertake shortly. Using the working notes space below, define the subject, scope and the time frame of your project. Don't forget: your project has to be within the decision accountabilities of you and/or other participants in the project.

_____
_____
_____
_____
_____
_____
_____
_____
_____
_____
_____
_____
_____
_____
_____
_____
_____
_____
_____

It also means that any interrogations you make of your data and any questions you ask (in particular the pivotal question, see Chapter 4) are relevant to your aim

– if you have the wrong entity then you may have the wrong question answered. It's best to get your entity right at the start.

Another reason for starting with the entity is to ensure that the project is within the decision accountability or scope of responsibility of the participants in the project – for example, you and your boss – in order that your recommendations can be put into action.

Think about one of your job projects and do the exercise opposite.

Defining the aim; not the journey

Once you have defined your entity you now need to define your aim. The aim is what you want to achieve. Think of this as the aspirational end point of all your hard work in a project.

An end point is not a strategy, a tactic, a set of decisions and so on. All of these are events in the process of working the project and if done well then they will lead to achieving the aim.

YOUR EXERCISE

Take the entity that you defined on the previous page. For this project, define the aim by showing focus, clearly stated end states and the time frame. Don't forget to start your aim with 'to be' and to check your aim against the entity. Does it look integrated?

_____
_____
_____
_____
_____
_____
_____
_____
_____
_____
_____
_____
_____
_____
_____
_____
_____

By its nature, an end point should be an aspiration – a stretching but realistic achievement. If the aim is stretching then it will ensure that you take into account all the possibilities you have – set it too low and it will limit your project.

Here is an example of a well defined aim: 'to be the brand leader or strong number two in every market we operate in within five years'. You can see in this example of an aim that I have started with 'to be', because this keeps me focused. Then I include an end state such as 'brand leader'. Finally, I include the time frame.

The aim should always integrate with the entity. For example, if you and other participants in the project are directly accountable for market leadership then the aim can reflect this. If you are not directly accountable then the aim is unrealistic for you.

Definitions of success; a shared vision of the future

It is important for all stakeholders to be aligned around the aim. Definitions of success help articulate the tangible indicators of delivery of the aspirational end state.

YOUR EXERCISE

Take your previous project. List out the main pre-set objectives of the project. It is likely that these objectives have been agreed with your boss and are SMART objectives. It is possible that a project has no pre-set objectives, so don't create them just for the sake of it.

———————————
———————————
———————————
———————————
———————————
———————————
———————————
———————————
———————————
———————————
———————————
———————————
———————————
———————————
———————————
———————————
———————————
———————————

Pre-set objectives; targets from a higher authority

Now for your third step in the SCQuARE process. An important consideration that you must take into account is the existence of objectives that have been agreed – known as pre-set objectives.

Are pre-set objectives the aim? No, the aim is the stretching end point and pre-set objectives are 'milestones' that you will achieve as you proceed towards the aim. For example, the aim is 'to win the war' and a pre-set objective could be 'to win a battle' in the war.

Invariably, pre-set objectives are numerical goals that management demands. For example, 20% growth in pre-tax profit or compliance with a budget. Pre-set objectives make up the daily nature of management. For example 'management by objectives' using SMART objectives (Specific, Measureable, Achievable, Realistic and Timed) are fundamental management tools.

In the main, pre-set objectives are agreed between the various participants and as such they must be taken into account if they affect and/or constrain a project. There is no point in having a worthy and stretching aim if by achieving this aim you drive a bus through your boss's objectives – definitely the wrong career move!

'... which brings me to surmise ...'

Create the Setting; establish the context of the plan

Your next step is to start to create the setting – an analysis based upon all the relevant and important positive information, truths and sound accepted judgements that provide a context.

The Setting generates a thorough understanding of where you are now and where you were. Information in the setting has a distinct 'positive' character – for example, strengths, assets, values, successes and unique skills. To ascertain what fits within the setting, ask yourself the question 'is this fact or set of circumstances an aid to delivering your aim?' If the answer is 'yes', then it fits under setting. If, the answer is 'no – it is a barrier to my aim' then it will fit under the consequence section.

Clearly, the context of your project could be very broad and very complex. Nonetheless, you need to create an understandable situation. To do this, I would recommend two simple techniques.

First, use checklists of all factors that could be relevant. These checklists could be:

Factors about the setting
performance factors
political factors
historical factors
organisational factors
(and so on)

Factors about successes
organisational successes
product successes
individual successes
significant results
(and so on)

Factors about strengths
resource strengths
skill strengths
brand strengths
marketing strengths
(and so on)

Secondly, keep testing every fact in your checklist results for relevancy and importance against the aim you have set for your project. The more you test, the more you will see the situation clearly. In effect, creating the context is an iterative process – going around and around until the fundamentals become very clear.

Positive '. . . so what?'

At this stage in the process we have an entity, an aim, possibly a set of pre-set objectives and facts that underpin a setting. We have also conducted some

STARTING WITH THE SETTING

analysis by assessing our facts for relevancy and importance against the aim.

We can now use positive 'so what?' This is very useful because it makes the interpretation of groups of facts more meaningful by ensuring that all your facts, truths and sound judgements are giving a positive interpretation in relation to your aim.

Let me give you an example of how powerful this can be. Imagine that you are the sales director of an insurance company aiming for profitable market share growth.

When you have created your setting you will have a group of facts indicating *'we have 10 offices covering every region of the country and we have been established for 30 years'.*

A low value interpretation of these facts would be *'we are a long-standing company with a strong infrastructure'*. This interpretation immediately leads to the comment 'so what, tell me something I don't know?'

However, imagine I positively interpreted these same facts as 'we are easily accessible to our customers and our heritage says we can be trusted'. Now we

YOUR EXERCISE

Take your project from previous pages and create the context based upon the facts. Try to group your facts together. These groupings are more meaningful and will aid your interpretation. Check all the facts for relevancy and importance against the aim.

29

can get excited about this statement and it is immediately and significantly more useful.

Follow this process. For each group of facts in your setting ask the question 'so what?' in relation to the aim and the entity.

Summary

Shortly, I would like you to read a case study and also start a real project based upon your job. However, before this practical work I would like to summarise this chapter.

After you have identified the issue, your next step is to define the entity by stating the subject, scope and time frame of your project. Don't forget, your entity has to be well defined because it channels your data collection and analysis onto only relevant and important matters. An entity must be in the accountability of the participants.

Your next step is to define the aim. The aim is what you want to achieve and it is the end point of your work. Remember: the aim should be stretching. An aim generally starts with 'to be' and it contains

YOUR EXERCISE

Take your context from the previous page. For each grouping of facts ask the question 'so what?' Try to provide all your groups with a positive interpretation. If it is not positive, it should be examined in the consequences.

_____
_____
_____
_____
_____
_____
_____
_____
_____
_____
_____
_____
_____
_____
_____
_____
_____
_____

some sort of end state and/or measure. It also has a specified time frame that integrates with the entity.

Your next step is to consider any pre-set objectives that have been agreed. Not all your projects will have pre-set objectives, but if they are present then they will generally be SMART objectives.

Your next step is to create the setting of all the relevant and important facts that underpin it. Generally, this will involve you investigating your setting and making lists of positive facts that aid the delivery of your aim, and then grouping these facts.

Your final step is to create a positive interpretation of these facts in your setting. Keep asking the question 'so what?' If you are not satisfied by your answers then keep going with your interpretations until you are.

Case study

I have designed the case study below to bring out all the elements of using the SCQuARE principles. The case study is based upon a real situation but the identities have been disguised.

At the end of each chapter I will develop the case further using the ideas and processes of that chapter. Here, I will focus on the setting or the **'S'** in the SCQuARE mnemonic.

First, I will present the case study as a reading narrative so that you have an overview. I will then re-present it in two columns.

CASE STUDY

How can John get everyone on the same page?

Standard Products Limited (SPL) is a major manufacturer and distributor of high quality chocolate products in the UK market. It has three divisions, Supermarkets, Newsagents and the Family Grocers Division (FGD).

John Barnwell has recently been appointed to run the FGD. He was looking forward to his new job knowing that FGD was the market leader in all of its market segments and John felt he could continue this leadership by maintaining the highly competitive strength of market and distribution coverage that FGD enjoyed.

Upon starting his new job he was surprised to find that the main board had recently accepted the findings of management consultants who were recommending that direct store deliveries (a major strength in John's mind) should cease in order to save costs of £20 m over three years and release funds for stronger brand building activities.

Of the £20 m, John had to find £15 m of cost savings by ceasing the large number of frequent small deliveries that the FGD made. John had two weeks to come up with an acceptable plan – an immense task that he would relish.

John immediately called his management team together and started to gather the facts. He summarised these to be:

STARTING WITH THE SETTING

CASE STUDY

Finance reported that:

Last year's revenue was £125 m on case sales of 6 m, a growth of 8%.

This performance delivered profit before tax of £20 m.

This performance was good compared with the rest of the group – which was flat.

30% of SPL volume was derived from FGD.

Next year's approved budget would be volume growth at 8% to 6.5 m cases and profits before tax to grow to £22 m.

Market intelligence stated that:

Walkers, the main competitor with 15% market share, had renewed its main fleet contracts.

Walkers were also taking out full-page trade adverts to publicise its levels of customer service.

Sales operations highlighted that:

The market was highly fragmented, with an estimated 31,250 shops, 90% of which were independently owned.

FGD had their products sold in over 25,500 shops (80% concentrated in the major cities), of which 22,000 were serviced by the direct store deliveries.

Nationwide availability was recognised as the key to success.

The market was serviced by 10 major competitive suppliers through direct deliveries, wholesalers, merchandisers and 'cash and carry' warehouses.

Alternative routes to market existed but there was significant variability of quality and coverage and FGD had had very few dealings with these alternatives.

Patel wholesalers covered 70% of the market.

CASE STUDY

'Cash and carry' warehouses were nationwide but would only do business on their terms and gave no guarantees of sales volumes and were generally not prepared to be loyal to suppliers. Merchandising companies were also servicing the market – the best being Rhonda mobile merchandising, which was nationwide and had the potential for 10% of national sales.

Marketing assessed that:

The total market for FGD was currently worth £500m in value.

FGD was the market leader with a share of 25% with a growth forecast to 26%.

This performance was good compared with the rest of the group – which was 18%.

Market growth was forecast to be low at 2%.

In the left-hand column below, you have the narrative again. In the right-hand column you have the factors being brought out so that you can follow my analysis.

Follow John as he uses the SCQuARE process to get to grips with this risky problem. He starts his analysis with the **'S'** in the mnemonic – his main task is to define the entity, aim and create the setting by focusing on positive factors. Please note, not all positive factors have to be used in a setting, only those relevant to the entity under review.

CASE NARRATIVE

Standard Products Limited (SPL) is a major manufacturer and distributor of high quality chocolate products in the UK market. It has three divisions, Supermarkets, Newsagents and the Family Grocers Division (FGD).

CASE ANALYSIS

FOR THE SETTING

John Barnwell has recently been appointed to run the FGD. He was looking forward to his new job knowing that FGD was the brand leader in all of its market segments and John felt he could continue this leadership by maintaining the highly competitive strength of market and distribution coverage that FGD enjoyed.

Upon starting his new job he was surprised to find that the main board had recently accepted the findings of management consultants who were recommending that direct store deliveries (a major strength in John's mind) should cease in order to save costs of £20 m over three years and release funds for stronger brand building activities.

Of the £20 m, John had to find £15 m of cost savings by ceasing the large number of frequent small deliveries that the FGD made. John had two weeks to come up with an acceptable plan – an immense task that he would relish.

John immediately called his management team together and started to gather the facts and he summarised these to be:

Finance reported that:

Last year's revenue was £125 m on case sales of 6 m, a growth of 8%.

Entity
The Family Grocers Division.
Aim
To continue to be the brand leader in all market segments.

Pre-set objective 1
To save £15 m of distribution costs over three years.

FGD performance fact 1
Last year's revenue was £125 m on case sales of 6 m, a growth of 8%.

This performance delivered profit before tax of £20 m.

This performance was good compared with the rest of the group – which was flat.

30% of SPL volume is derived from FGD.

Next year's approved budget would be volume growth at 8% to 6.5 m cases and profits before tax to grow to £22 m.

Market intelligence stated that:

Walkers, the main competitor with 15% market share, had renewed its main fleet contracts.

Walkers were also taking out full-page trade adverts to publicise its levels of customer service.

Sales operations highlighted that:

The market was highly fragmented, with an estimated 31,250 shops, 90% of which were independently owned.

FGD had their products sold in over 25,500 shops (80% concentrated in the major cities), of which 22,000 were serviced by the direct store deliveries.

Nationwide availability was recognised as the key to success.

The market was serviced by 10 major competitive suppliers through direct

FGD performance fact 2

30% of SPL volume derived from FGD.

Pre-set objective 2

Volume growth at 8% to 6.5 m cases.

Pre-set objective 3

Profits to grow by 10% to £22 m.

FGD market fact 1

31,250 shops nationwide.

FGD market fact 2

90% independently owned.

FGD distribution fact 1

25,500 shops, 80% concentrated in 20 cities.

FGD distribution fact 2

22,000 serviced by direct store deliveries.

Market supply fact 1

Serviced by 10 major suppliers.

deliveries, wholesalers, merchandisers and 'cash and carry' warehouses.

Alternative routes to market existed but there was significant variability of quality and coverage and FGD had had very few dealings with these alternatives.

Patel wholesalers covered 70% of the market.

'Cash and carry' warehouses were nationwide but would only do business on their terms and gave no guarantees of sales volumes and were generally not prepared to be loyal to suppliers.

Merchandising service companies were also servicing the market – the best being Rhonda mobile merchandising, which was nationwide and had the potential for 10% of national sales.

Marketing assessed that:

The total market for FGD is currently worth £500m in value.

FGD was the market leader with a market share of 25% with a growth forecast to 26%.

This performance was good compared with the rest of the group – which was 18%.

Market growth is forecast to be low at 2%.

Market supply fact 2
Four different distribution channels.

FGD market fact 3
Total market worth £500m.

FGD performance fact 4
FGD market share at 25% better than group – which is 18%.

John created a summary of the setting with positive interpretation on the main facts (see overleaf).

SUMMARY OF FACTS	POSITIVE INTERPRETATION
Entity	
The Family Grocers Division	
Aim	
To continue to be the brand leader in all its market segments	To be profitable number 1
Pre-set objective 1	
£15m cost savings	
Pre-set objective 2	
Annual volume to grow 8% to 6.5m cases	
Pre-set objective 3	
PBT to grow by 10% to £22m	Planning for stretching growth
FGD market fact 1	
31,250 shops nationwide	
FGD market fact 2	
90% independently owned	
FGD market fact 3	
Total market worth £500m	Large market with fragmented ownership
Market supply fact 1	
10 major suppliers	
Market supply fact 2	
Four different distribution channels	Multiple suppliers and routes to market
FGD distribution fact 1	
25,500 shops (80% in cities)	
FGD distribution fact 2	
22,000 serviced by direct store deliveries	Wide availability driven by direct deliveries
FGD performance fact 1	
Last year's revenue was £125m on case sales of 6m, a growth of 8%	
FGD performance fact 2	
30% of SPL volume derived from FGD	
FGD performance fact 3	
FGD market share at 25% better than group – which was 18%	FGD are the star performer in the Group

YOUR PROJECT

Starting below you will find work sheets that will guide you to complete a project using SCQuARE. Doing this is very important because it will reinforce all the principles of SCQuARE and it is essential to maximise your learning.

Choose your project with care. It should be based upon your current job and it could be just about to start – the more real and timely the project you choose, the better it will be for your learning.

The project you choose will be continuous throughout the book. Here you will start with the setting – the **'S'** in the SCQuARE mnemonic.

At the end of each subsequent chapter you will pick up the project again and develop it further.

Define the entity

What is the subject?

What is the scope?

What is the time frame?

Is the project within your decision accountabilities?

Define the aim to achieve . . .

What is the aspirational end point?

What are the measures or definitions of success of this end point?

What is the time frame of this end point?

Are there any pre-set objectives?

Create the setting

What are the main relevant and important facts that underpin the setting for your project?

_____

_____

_____

_____

_____

_____

_____

_____

_____

What are the positive factors that will lead to achieving the aim or that you want to build on?

_____

_____

_____

_____

_____

_____

_____

_____

_____

_____

_____

_____

_____

_____

_____

_____

YOUR PROJECT

Setting continued . . .

Positive 'so what?'

Interpret the main groups of facts in the most positive way to give powerful meaning

Ask 'so what?' of all the groups of facts

'Just think about that move you're about to make Darren – have you any idea what you're getting yourself into!'

Logical consequences are the scarecrows of the fools and
the beacons of wise men

Thomas Huxley

CHAPTER 3

UNDERSTANDING THE CONSEQUENCES

In the last chapter I explained the importance of your aim and its setting – this is your start point. I now want to take you on the next steps of your journey with SCQuARE – exploring the '**C**' in the mnemonic.

Exploring '**C**' always starts with questions about changes, complications and consequences. Changes can also include new opportunities. What happens if things change? What happens if nothing changes? Will this factor complicate matters? What are the consequences of these changes? How will I cope with these consequences?

As you can see, all of these questions are 'interrogating' the factors in your setting to ensure that all of the consequences that could affect the achievement of your aim are fully exposed and then resolved.

Interrogating the Setting

In the last chapter you created the setting – this was the first stage of your analysis, based upon all the relevant and important positive facts, truths and sound accepted judgements that underpin a situation. You can use this setting as a start point for your second stage of analysis – the interrogation. Actually, as you make progress you will see that new factors begin to emerge to give added dimensions and depth to your setting. Don't worry about these new factors, they are increasing the quality of your analysis and your end results so they must be taken into account – just add them to your lists and interrogate them later.

To conduct the interrogation follow this simple process.

What has changed?

Study your setting and take each factor or group of factors in turn. Pay particular attention to all those facts and groups of facts that you powerfully enhanced by using positive 'so what?' interpretation.

'What has changed?' questions . . .

Interrogate each and every factor and/or group of factors in your setting by asking these questions:

Has this factor changed?
What caused this change?
When did this change occur?
Is this a positive or negative change?
What are the consequences of this change?
Can I cope with these consequences?
Has this change exposed a major risk?

What happens if this factor has not changed?
What are the consequences of lack of change?
Can I cope with these consequences?
Has this lack of change exposed a major risk?
Should I take into account any new factors?

YOUR EXERCISE

Take your exercise setting from the previous chapter, and for the main groups of factors interrogate them using the main questions above. Continue until you are confident that you have identified all the consequences of change and/or lack of change.

_____
_____
_____
_____
_____
_____
_____
_____
_____

First, focus on 'what has changed?' by repeatedly asking penetrating questions until the consequences of any changes are fully understood. The main questions are shown in the exercise box opposite.

For example, if your market share – as shown in your setting – is now beginning to decline then this could be a negative change with major adverse consequences. Equally, a market share that has not increased as expected could be a sign of lack of competitiveness and this lack of change has adverse consequences. What are these consequences?

What could change?

Secondly, focus on 'what could change?' by asking penetrating questions repeatedly until the consequences of the potential change are fully understood. The main questions are shown in the exercise box opposite.

For example, in the last chapter I used an example of a firm having 10 offices covering every region of the country and I used a positive interpretation: 'we are easily accessible to our customers'.

'What could change?' questions . . .

Interrogate each and every factor and/or group of factors in your setting by asking these questions.

Could this factor change?
If so, what would create this change?
When would this change occur?
Is this a positive or negative change?
What are the consequences of this change?
Could I cope with these consequences?
Does this change expose a major risk?

What happens if this factor does not change?
What are the consequences of lack of change?
Could I cope with these consequences?
Does this lack of change expose a major risk?
Should I take into account any new factors?

YOUR EXERCISE

Build on your exercise by interrogating your setting using the main questions above. Continue until you are confident that you have identified all the consequences of potential change.

_____
_____
_____
_____
_____
_____
_____
_____
_____
_____

As I interrogate, I see that the main change could be a change in the demographic structure in the locations of the offices and this would be a negative change with very risky consequences to the firm's customer base.

What about complications?

Thirdly, I need to look for any factors that expose complications, barriers, problems or limiting factors that may interfere with my ability to achieve my aim.

For example, my competitor always spends more on advertising than I do and this is a complication to my strategy and plans.

Importantly, this is not change *per se* because any new situation will be relatively the same as the old situation – but it is critical to my analysis!

Of course you could have the situation whereby your competitor always spends more than you but this year there was a doubling in expenditure – and you can't match this increase! Now your advertising expenditure has become a limiting factor.

'What about complications?' questions . . .

Interrogate each and every factor and/or group of factors in your setting by asking these questions.

Could this factor complicate my plans?
If so, what are the negative consequences?
Could I cope with these consequences?
Does this complication expose a major risk?

What happens if I resolve this complication?
Will the resolution expose more consequences?
Could I cope with these new consequences?

What are the limiting factors?
Do these limiting factors have a consequence?
Could I cope with these limiting factors?

Should I take into account any new factors?

YOUR EXERCISE

Build on your exercise by interrogating your setting using the main questions above. Continue until you are confident that you have identified all the consequences of any complications

_____
_____
_____
_____
_____
_____
_____

Clearly, complications disguising limiting factors are crucial to your ideas and plans – so search hard for them and give them proper attention.

Remember, not all changes are bad news, they may indeed highlight opportunities which need to be exploited. These may well generate options – more of which shortly.

The main questions are shown in the exercise box opposite.

More about Consequences

The underlying theme of this chapter so far is the importance of consequences – for example, if something changes what are the downside risks of this change? Could it be disastrous?

It is now important to understand how iterative the analysis process is. You start with a clear aim and a setting. As you interrogate, new factors emerge which can change the setting and, indeed, refine the aim even further.

As you proceed around the iterations a clearer picture emerges as you see the fundamentals of all the issues. The final picture takes its true meaning when you fully understand all the consequences of factors in your situation.

In fact, this reminds me to say 'if you don't understand the consequences you don't understand the issues'. A truism? Maybe, but how many times have you seen great mistakes made because a person and/or team just see the factors and then assume a solution? If they had pursued the factors more thoroughly then they would have exposed the hidden consequences and risks.

I would now like to introduce you to a very powerful technique that ensures you fully understand all the issues because you fully understand all the consequences and the causes of these consequences. In particular, as you will see, it helps to make clear what real options you may have and their outcomes – including the option and outcome of doing nothing!

The causal chain

During the interrogation I focused you onto the consequences and in particular the issue of whether you could cope with or live with these consequences.

Now, the business reality is this. If you can't live with the consequences of a factor then you have to fix the cause that is creating the adverse consequences. Even if you can't fix the cause you still need to avoid or minimise the negative consequences in some way.

'Sorry boss, I'm afraid your car was involved in a causal chain with an unfortunate consequence.'

In effect, I have created a direct link between a cause and a consequence and if I know the cause or causes of a consequence then I have the best chances of finding a fix. This linkage is the 'causal chain' – for every change or complication with a consequence there is a direct link to a cause.

You can see this idea in the diagram on the right. This is the basic unit of a causal chain. More complex situations would create more complex causal chains – but the approach is the same.

For example, a marketing manager is noticing a loss in market share and profit for an important product – the consequence of something. This is due to a change in product sales, which are falling. The cause of this is that the product is at the end of its life cycle. You could continue your analysis and find that there are other causes, such as low investment or product development

delays and so on. Or you could look at other consequences and in particular look for the downside risk – the disaster consequence.

Of course, most situations that you will deal with are more complicated. And you can see why this happens! Every change or complication has consequences, and these have causes. Importantly, in a more complex situation it is possible to have a number of changes or complications in a causal chain system and it is possible that these changes or complications have a number of consequences and these may have a number of causes.

Equally, a consequence of a change could be the cause of another change and so on. Although this may sound quite complicated it is in fact very easy to see how it works. Let me take you through a more complicated situation. In fact, you will be a little familiar with this example because it is based on the Family Grocers Division (FGD) case study – I've borrowed John Barnwell for a few minutes!

You will remember that John has to deal with a situation where the main board have decided to cease direct deliveries. This represents a major change in how FGD does business.

In the following diagram you will see the situation that John is dealing with – you will find the 'change' box in the centre of the causal chain diagram. As John analyses the causes he finds that the first level of cause is the potential reduction in profits that could occur if the matter is not dealt with. However, the causes below this are very important. John can 'drill down' in his analysis and find two 'root' causes – a fragmented and mature market and economic uncertainty. These are 'root' causes because they are the absolute basic causes of the problem. This is the general rule – pursue all the causes in the linked system. Stop when the causes start to fall outside your control. For example, you are unlikely to be able to influence government legislation.

Let us follow the causal chain and see what we learn. The root cause 'fragmented and mature market' creates a 'change' and three 'complications'. First,

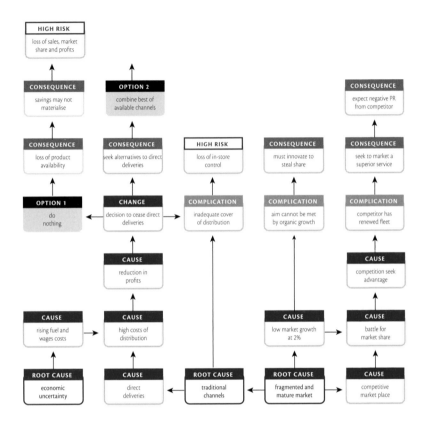

because the market is mature it has traditional distribution channels mainly based upon direct deliveries (a major strength for FGD). In combination with another root cause 'economic uncertainty', producing rising fuel and wage costs, the cost of direct distribution is rising and will cause a reduction in profits – this is just a matter of time. The main board make the risky but very necessary decision to cease direct deliveries to maintain these profits and also create stimulation for channel innovation. It is John's role to be the innovator.

Clearly, the consequence of this change if John does nothing could be loss of product availability and that the cost savings do not materialise. John then faces the very high risk consequence of loss of sales, market share and profits.

Meanwhile, the traditional distribution channels mean that if you cease direct deliveries then the alternative distribution methods are fragmented and inadequate, for example no single alternative distributor fully covers the marketplace and this is a major issue that John has to deal with. The consequence is that John needs to

'Wheeee! down we go . . . and a clear consequence is that we will now all lose our jobs . . . any questions?'

reorganise how he gets his products to the market without losing sales and in-store control.

Also, the mature market means that the market growth rate is low and this is a complication that John needs to handle. The consequence is that there are low opportunities for organic growth and this means that any stretching objectives cannot be met by organic growth alone. John will have to innovate to steal market share.

Finally, because the market is mature it is also very competitive, with all market suppliers fighting for share of a low growth marketplace. This fight for market share is a complication and John knows that his competitors will react aggressively to whatever plans he puts in place.

Clearly, John has to do something. His options are few. He has the option of doing nothing and the option of exploiting the third party distribution opportunities by combining the best channels that are available to him after the direct deliveries cease.

Why does John think he's got the option of doing nothing? Common sense tells him that he hasn't but he's learnt from long experience that this option should always be left on the table – you'll be surprised at how many times your best option proves to have been to do nothing!

You will notice on the causal chain diagram that there are two exit links and John intends to continue his causal chain analysis to see the further consequences of his options – see next chapter.

In the following pages you will see how John identified his consequences to changes and complications.

Summary

The '**S**' and '**C**' of the SCQuARE mnemonic are the two connected analysis stages of SCQuARE – together they represent your foundation for action.

In chapter two, covering the '**S**' in the SCQuARE mnemonic, you identified the entity which described the subject, covering scope and time frame. Then you defined the aim – the end point of your work. With the entity and aim in mind you then identified all the relevant, important, positive factors that were contained in the setting. Finally, you used the concept of positive 'so what?' to interpret the factors in the setting and give greater strength and positive focus to your analysis.

In chapter three, the '**C**' in the SCQuARE mnemonic, you introduced the idea of interrogating your factors (starting with those in your setting) to look for factors that have changed or will change, including new opportunities, and in particular you were focused on the consequences of these changes in relation to the achievement of your aim. You did the same for complications and/or limiting factors.

This leads you to your current point in your journey. Each consequence has a cause or causes and these causes have to be thoroughly understood if you are to find a fix to avoid the consequences – this is the message of the causal chain.

I'll now update the Family Grocers Division case study and show you how we bring out the consequences to any changes and complications – the '**C**' in the SCQuARE mnemonic.

The case narrative in the left-hand column is repeated from the previous chapter. The right-hand column is for use in the analysis.

HOW CAN JOHN GET EVERYONE ON THE SAME PAGE?

CASE NARRATIVE

Standard Products Limited (SPL) is a major manufacturer and distributor of high quality chocolate products in the UK market. It has three divisions, Supermarkets, Newsagents and the Family Grocers Division (FGD).

John Barnwell has recently been appointed to run the FGD. He was looking forward to his new job knowing that FGD was the market leader in all of its market segments and John felt he could continue this leadership by maintaining the highly competitive strength of market and distribution coverage that FGD enjoyed.

Upon starting his new job he was surprised to find that the main board had just recently accepted the findings of management consultants who were recommending that direct store deliveries (a major strength in John's mind) should cease in order to save costs of £20 m over three years and release funds for much stronger brand building activities.

Of the £20 m, John had to find £15 m of cost savings by ceasing the large number of frequent small drops that the FGD made. John had two weeks to come up with an acceptable plan – an immense task that he would relish.

CASE ANALYSIS

FOR CONSEQUENCES

Change 1
The board of SPL have decided to cease direct store deliveries in order to save costs of £20 m and release funds for stronger brand building activities.

Consequence A
Savings of £15 m for FGD could be nullified by the potential loss of FGD business that has been built around nationwide availability and the servicing of nearly 90% of customers by direct deliveries.

CASE NARRATIVE

John immediately called his management team together and started to gather the facts and he summarised these to be:

Finance reported that:

Last year's revenue was £125 m on case sales of 6.2 m, a growth of 8%.

This performance delivered profit before tax of £20 m.

This performance was good compared with the rest of the group – which was flat.

30% of SPL volume is derived from FGD.

Next year's approved budget would be volume growth at 8% to 6.5 m cases and profits before tax to grow to £22 m.

Market intelligence stated that:

Walkers, the main competitor with 15% market share, had renewed its main fleet contracts.

Walkers were also taking out full-page trade adverts to publicise its levels of customer service.

Sales operations highlighted that:

The market was highly fragmented, with an estimated 31,250 shops, 90% of which were independently owned.

CASE ANALYSIS

Complication 1

Walkers, the main competitor with 15% market share, had renewed their main fleet contracts and they were also taking out full-page trade adverts to publicise their levels of customer service.

Consequence A

They will almost certainly mount an aggressive campaign accusing FGD of deserting the family grocers business, aiming to steal the FGD customer base.

CASE NARRATIVE

FGD had their products sold in over 25,500 shops (80% concentrated in the major cities), of which 22,000 were serviced by the direct store deliveries.

Nationwide availability was recognised as the key to success.

The market was serviced by 10 major competitive suppliers through direct deliveries, wholesalers, merchandisers and 'cash and carry' warehouses.

Alternative routes to market existed but there was significant variability of quality and coverage and FGD had had very few dealings with these alternatives.

Patel wholesalers cover 70% of the market.

'Cash and carry' warehouses were nationwide but would only do business on their terms and gave no guarantees of sales volumes and were generally not prepared to be loyal to suppliers.

Merchandising service companies were also servicing the market – the best being Rhonda mobile merchandising, which was nationwide and had the potential for 10% of national sales.

Marketing assessed that:

The total market for FGD was currently worth £500 m in value.

FGD was the market leader with a share of 25% with a growth forecast to 26%.

CASE ANALYSIS

Complication 2

No alternative single distributor offers the same coverage as FGD's current direct deliveries – Patel wholesalers only cover 70%, 'cash and carry' warehouses demand promotional allowances without giving guarantees and merchandisers were currently unused but had some potential.

Consequence A

Some form of combination of distributors will be required in order to maintain current availability of FGD products.

Consequence B

There could be some loss in relationships and loss of in-store control.

CASE NARRATIVE

This performance was good compared with the rest of the group – which was 18%.

Market growth was forecast to be low at 2%.

CASE ANALYSIS

Complication 3

Market growth is low at 2%.

Consequence A

FGD cannot meet its stretching aim and pre-set objectives by relying on organic market growth alone so it must innovate and steal share.

To view John's FGD case analysis on a causal chain, refer back to the diagram on page 52.

YOUR PROJECT

Start with the factors in your setting. As you go through your interrogation don't worry if you find new factors, just add them to your list.

What has changed?

Use this checklist

Has this factor changed?

What created this change?

When did this change occur?

Is this a positive or negative change?

What are the consequences of this change?

Can I cope with these consequences?

Has this change exposed a major risk?

What could change?

Use this checklist:

Could this factor change?

If so, what would create this change?

When would this change occur?

Is this a positive or negative change?

What are the consequences of this change?

Could I cope with these consequences?

Does this change expose a major risk?

What happens if this factor did not change?

What are the consequences of lack of change?

Could I cope with these consequences?

Does this lack of change expose a major risk?

Should I take into account any new factors?

Here you have the opportunity to continue your project. Just follow the instructions

_____

_____

_____

_____

_____

_____

_____

_____

_____

_____

_____

_____

_____

_____

_____

_____

_____

_____

_____

_____

_____

_____

_____

_____

_____

_____

YOUR PROJECT

Any complications?

Use this checklist:

Could this factor complicate my plans?

If so, what are the negative consequences?

Could I cope with these consequences?

Does this complication expose a major risk?

What happens if I resolve this complication?

Will the resolution expose more consequences?

Could I cope with these new consequences?

What are the limiting factors?

Do these limiting factors have a consequence?

Could I cope with these limiting factors?

Should I take into account any new factors?

When you have finished your workings, use the template opposite to create your causal chain diagram.

Causal Chain template

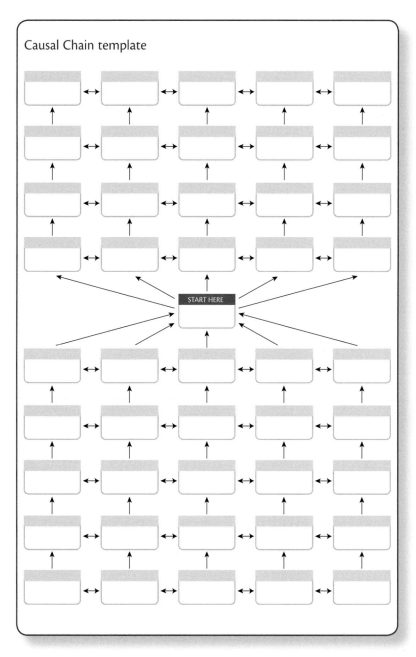

START HERE

YOUR PROJECT

A problem well stated
is a problem half solved.

JOHN DEWEY

CHAPTER 4

DEFINING THE PIVOTAL QUESTION

By the end of the last chapter I had arrived at the point where I had fully investigated a situation and had at my 'fingertips' a lot of relevant and important information – including all causes and their consequences.

For example, I had a clear subject, scope and time frame making up the entity. Importantly, I had a clear aim in a setting of positive factors. For each factor, I had interrogated to find the consequences to any changes and complications and any major risks. Finally, I had an idea of the options that were available that could lead to achieving my aim.

In principle, there is nothing more I can do in order to analyse my situation. Now, I have to find answers, create plans and persuade others of my ideas. Analysis job done – the synthesis starts here!

And this starts with the next step in your journey with SCQuARE.

To explore the '**Qu**' in the mnemonic – the pivotal question.

What does 'Pivotal Question' mean?

The pivotal question is so important to the SCQuARE process that I am going to spend a minute on defining exactly what I mean by the 'pivotal question'. If you refer to your trusty dictionary you will see that 'pivot' is simply defined as 'a crucial point upon which things turn' and 'question' is defined as 'that which demands an answer'. There are other more subtle definitions but these best express my understanding.

In my mind, the 'pivotal question' is the single question upon which all the issues and facts turn and where the best answer is found.

This understanding is important. For example, in the Family Grocers Division (FGD) case study, John has arrived at the point where he has important factors and consequences that make up his problem. How can he proceed with confidence knowing that he will find the best answers and solutions to his problem?

'Meet our new delivery fleet. . . . it has a tiny carbon footprint!!'

Of course, like all other managers, he could jump to a surprising conclusion – 'yes, that's what I'll do!' – and congratulate himself on his creativity and thank himself for all the hard work and years of experience.

As useful as this approach can be on occasions, SCQuARE wisely counsels caution. Too many times solutions are based on assumptions, false experience, 'motherhood' type ideas, the politics of what will be acceptable, the expediency of time pressures and a myriad of other cloudy reasons.

SCQuARE says 'no' – you take all your output from your analysis so far and subject it to focused reflection and scrutiny and then real creativity. SCQuARE asks what is the 'pivotal question' that all your important factors turn upon and then signifies the best way forward.

This is why the pivotal question is so important. It reminds you to exercise caution yet focuses you onto finding the right answer. In effect, all the directions you take towards the achievement of your aim.

The principles of the Pivotal Question

Now that you can see what I mean by a pivotal question, let me show you the main principles of building the pivotal question from scratch.

The **first principle** is that the pivotal question is a real question that signifies and demands an answer. By 'signifying' I mean that the question contains a main action (at the strategic level) that answers the question and that will lead to my aim. It contains no details of a plan but signifies the broad nature of the plan.

In effect, when I state my pivotal question to an audience, the audience have an idea of how I'm going to proceed later. This is my first step in persuading others of my ideas. If I can't communicate my main action effectively at this point (using common language) then I will not be able to persuade others of the details of my plan at a later point.

For example, John in the FGD case study could start to create a pivotal question and ask, 'how can we deliver our sales target and overcome our distribution problems?' Immediately you can see what John has done – he's

'It's all starting to become clear ...'

only restated the problem and he is no further forward. He should ask, 'how can we combine the best of our alternative distribution options in order to meet our aim?' John has now stated within the pivotal question the main action he will take.

The **second principle** is that the pivotal question is a synthesis of all your analysis and the key conclusions you have reached at this point. It doesn't restate all of your analysis in detail, instead it succinctly summarises it into a question that all your important findings 'turn' on. Although the pivotal question is a proxy for the 'whole' analysis, it still needs to be succinct.

In fact, this is a difficult principle – your question needs to be succinct but represent the 'whole', it needs to be precise without stultifying interpretation and later creativity. Ultimately, the fullness of your question will dictate the fullness of your answer.

However difficult this matter is, the caveat is that if you miss an important issue in your analysis and its representation in your pivotal question, then your answer will be incomplete – miss a minor issue and you will recover later in the SCQuARE process, but miss a major issue and your plans will always be out of balance.

The **third principle** stems from the second principle. Getting the pivotal question right is an iterative process. Only in the simplest of matters will you get it right at the first attempt. Generally you will need many attempts to get a question that best represents the situation. Actually, the test of the final and best pivotal question lies in the understanding I outlined earlier in the chapter.

After many iterations (in a complex situation) the pivotal question is right if it 'demands an answer' and then 'signifies the answer'. This 'answer' is then tested (see next chapter – the '**A**' in the SCQuARE mnemonic) and if it survives this testing then the question is the right one – your granny used to say 'the proof of the pudding is in the eating'! The golden rule is to be persistent – rest assured, you will find the right pivotal question.

The **fourth principle** is to expect the process of creating the right question to take you back into your analysis of '**S**' and '**C**'. In a complex situation, if your first or early attempts generate a question that cannot be answered then it is not a pivotal question. In fact, you will find that you have found a new change or complication with a consequence. This (or these) will have to be taken into account.

Finally, **the fifth principle** is that the pivotal question is a 'bridge' to the future and you have to 'cross over' this 'bridge'. It signifies action that will lead to good results and achieving your aim. It signifies a strategy and a plan to take you into the future. It inspires you to move forward.

This fifth principle is probably the most important test of you – you need to exercise real leadership to take yourself and others 'across' your 'bridge'! The pivotal question is not just part of a technical process; it is a signifier of good leadership and represents the best that you can achieve.

Building the Pivotal Question

If these are the principles, what is the process we follow to create the pivotal question? Actually, the process is very simple and systematic but it does require your careful reflections.

SUMMARY OF PRINCIPLES

- The pivotal question is a real question that signifies and demands an answer.
- The pivotal question is a synthesis of all your analysis and the key conclusions you have reached.
- The fullness of your question dictates the fullness of your answer.
- Getting the pivotal question right is an iterative process.
- Expect the process of creating the pivotal question to take you back into your analysis of '**S**' and '**C**'.
- The pivotal question is a 'bridge' to the future and you have to 'cross over'.

As simple as the process is, it has taken many years to get it right. You may be familiar with the saying 'making the complex simple'; well this best represents the approach I have taken with clients worldwide in order to get the process simple but right.

I usually start with a generalised question:

'How can I take 'a main action' *to* 'overcome any issues'

and 'exploit any opportunities' *so that I will meet my*

'pre-set objectives' *and I will achieve my* 'stated aim'?

If I can systematically fill in the 'gaps' as it were, whilst bearing in mind the principles I mentioned previously, then I will arrive at the pivotal question – which can then be tested and refined by the iterative process. I have created a template that you can use to help fill in these gaps and I will show you this shortly. Before this, I need to develop a few ideas in more detail.

The first gap in the generalised question is '**a main action**' and this, you will recall, means an action (at the strategic level) that will lead to achieving my aim. Although it contains no details of a plan, it does signify the broad nature of the plan.

It is useful to refer to the FGD case study again. At the end of the last chapter John Barnwell had arrived at the point where his causal chain diagram showed that he had two options – do nothing or combine best of available channels (see the following diagram).

You can also see that John has now developed his causal chain diagram upwards to show the outcome of the two options he had. As expected, the consequence of doing nothing will be that he does not meet his aim. This is not a viable option.

Causal chain diagram for the Family Grocers Division

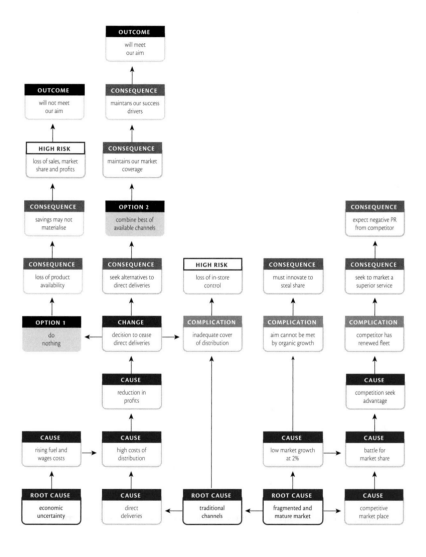

However, if he uses the best of the available channels and maintains the market coverage and in-store control and maintains his success drivers (and copes with negative PR from his main competitor) then he will meet his aim. Combining the best available channels is his main action. It is strategic, it has no details but it signifies the broad plan and it leads to his aim.

The second gap in the generalised question is 'overcome any issues'. Issues in this context can mean a number of things. It could be a barrier or a constraint that has to be overcome. It could mean a limiting factor or a major risk factor that has to be taken into account and overcome. It could mean a weakness or a threat that has to be neutralised and overcome. It could mean a complication or the results of a change that have to be overcome. In principle it can mean any 'negative' factor that is an impediment to progress towards an aim and therefore has to be overcome, neutralised, removed and avoided and so on.

As far as FGD is concerned John reflects on his findings. Bearing in mind that organic growth is a non-starter in relation to his aim, John concludes that there are five main issues that have to be overcome:

- The loss of product availability from ceasing direct deliveries.
- The threat of negative PR from the main competitor.
- The need to save £15m costs over three years.
- The loss of in-store control.
- Low market growth at 2%.

In John's mind, these issues are the main negative issues that describe his situation and these issues must be accounted for in the pivotal question.

The third gap in the generalised question is 'exploit any opportunities'. Opportunities in this context can mean a number of things. It could mean an opportunity or an innovation that could be realised. It could mean a strength or uniqueness that could be built upon. It could mean a positive interpretation or an imaginative difference that is compelling. It could mean a real benefit or an expected result that could be brought out. In principle, it can mean any 'positive' factor identified in the '**S**' and '**C**' that can be utilised in order to progress towards an aim and therefore has to be brought to the fore.

As far as FGD is concerned, John again reflects on his findings and concludes that there are two opportunities that should be brought out:

- The strengths of alternative distribution channels.
- Some reinvestment of the £15 m cost savings that should materialise.

In John's mind, these are the fundamental positive issues that describe his situation and therefore these issues must be recognised and accounted for in the pivotal question.

The fourth and fifth gaps in the generalised question are 'pre-set objectives' and 'stated aim'. These are directly taken from your findings in your setting – the '**S**' in the SCQuARE mnemonic.

In John's case, you will recall, he has done all his analysis and thinking on these factors in his setting and he has pre-set objectives of:

- Annual volume to grow by 8% to 6.5 m cases.
- PBT to grow by 10% to £22 m.
- £15 m cost savings.

and the stated aim of:

- To continue to be the brand leader in all market segments.

Again in John's mind, these represent his stretching measurements for the strategy he needs to develop and detail.

You can see here that a lot of information is going into the pivotal question. Again, you will recall that the pivotal question has to be the 'whole' matter but it also needs to be succinct and represent the 'turning point' of all the information. I have developed a template (opposite) that you can use to bring all your information together as a framework for the phrasing of the pivotal question – bearing in mind that in a complex situation you will need a number of attempts to get the question right.

To demonstrate the template I will use John's pivotal question. Importantly, John does not fill in this template from the top down but from the bottom up, i.e. the aim first. This is to remind John as he builds the question always to remain focused on the aim and if he notices an inconsistency in any matter as he proceeds from the bottom to the top, then that matter has to be dealt with before the pivotal question is completed.

You can see in the template opposite the full specification of John's pivotal question. You can think of this as the 'reference' pivotal question against which all future iterations of the question will be judged. Once John is happy with a final pivotal question then he will summarise this into a more succinct form for shorthand communication.

Summary

So far in this book I have covered the '**SCQu**' of the SCQuARE mnemonic. It has been a journey through analysis, the '**S**' and the '**C**', through to the start of the synthesis process, the '**Qu**'.

Each step so far has been bringing out layers of issues in more and more depth but because we are following a tried and tested process the complex is becoming more and more simple.

In this chapter you gained an understanding of the pivotal question – a single question which all issues and facts turn on. When answered, it shows you the best direction that will take you towards your aim. Not only does it show the right direction, it also reminds you that you must exercise caution – don't jump to conclusions too quickly.

Pivotal Question template

How can   [I/We/The Entity]   *The Family Grocers Division*

[Main action]   ***combine the best of alternative distribution options***

in order to Overcome: and Exploit:

the loss of product availability from   *alternative third party*
ceasing direct deliveries   *distributors*
[Issue]   [Opportunity]

the threat of negative PR   *some reinvestment of the £15m cost*
from main competitor   *savings*
[Issue]   [Opportunity]

the need to save £15m costs
over three years
[Issue]   [Opportunity]

the loss of in-store control

[Issue]   [Opportunity]

slow market growth

[Issue]   [Opportunity]

annual volume to grow by 8% to 6.5m cases
PBT to grow by 10% to £22m
To achieve   [Pre-set objectives]   *£15m cost savings*

to continue to be the brand leader in all its market segments

And/or   [Aim]

The pivotal question is based on certain principles. It must contain a main action, it must succinctly take into account all the main findings from your analysis and it must be a 'bridge' to the future. In a complex situation you will need a number of iterations before you have a pivotal question that you are happy with – be patient.

To start the synthesis you can use a generalised question. This will ask for a main action, issues to be overcome and opportunities for exploitation, and focus these onto your pre-set objectives and stated aim. To help you, you can use the pivotal question template that puts these requirements in the correct arrangement for your best results.

As you can see from this chapter, John is making good progress with his problem. I'll now update the case study for the pivotal question – the '**Qu**' in the SCQuARE mnemonic.

The case narrative in the left-hand column is repeated from the previous chapter. The right-hand column is for use in the analysis.

HOW CAN JOHN GET EVERYONE ON THE SAME PAGE?

John now begins the process of building the pivotal question into the template (see page 78).

CASE NARRATIVE

Standard Products Limited (SPL) is a major manufacturer and distributor of high quality chocolate products in the UK market. It has three divisions, Supermarkets, Newsagents and the Family Grocers Division (FGD).

John Barnwell has recently been appointed to run the FGD. He was looking forward to his new job knowing that FGD was the market leader in all of its market segments and John felt he could continue this leadership by maintaining the highly competitive strength of market and distribution coverage that FGD enjoyed.

Upon starting his new job he was surprised to find that the main board had just recently accepted the findings of management consultants who were recommending that direct store deliveries (a major strength in John's mind) should cease in order to save costs of £20 m over three years and release funds for stronger brand building activities.

Of the £20 m, John had to find £15 m of cost savings by ceasing the large number of frequent small drops that the FGD made. John had two weeks to come up with an acceptable plan – an immense task that he would relish.

John immediately called his management team together and started to gather the facts and he summarised these to be:

Finance reported that:

Last year's revenue was £125 m on case sales of 6.2 m, a growth of 8%.

CASE ANALYSIS

FOR THE PIVOTAL QUESTION

Entity
The Family Grocers Division.

Stated aim
To continue to be the brand leader in all market segments.

Pre-set objectives
Annual volume to grow by 8% to 6.5 m cases.
PBT to grow by 10% to £22 m.
£15 m cost savings.

A main negative to be overcome
The loss of product availability from ceasing direct deliveries.
A main negative to be overcome
The loss of relationships and in-store control.

A main negative to be overcome
The need to save £15 m costs.
A main positive to be exploited
Some reinvestment of the £15 m cost savings that should materialise.

CASE NARRATIVE

This performance delivered profit before tax of £20 m.

This performance was good compared with the rest of the group – which was flat.

30% of SPL volume is derived from FGD.

Next year's approved budget would be volume growth at 8% to 6.5 m cases and profits before tax to grow to £22 m.

Market intelligence stated that:

Walkers, the main competitor with 15% market share, had renewed its main fleet contracts.

Walkers were also taking out full-page trade adverts to publicise its levels of customer service.

Sales operations highlighted that:

The market was highly fragmented, with an estimated 31,250 shops, 90% of which were independently owned.

FGD had their products sold in over 25,500 shops (80% concentrated in the major cities), of which 22,000 were serviced by the direct store deliveries.

Nationwide availability was recognised as the key to success.

The market was serviced by 10 major competitive suppliers through direct deliveries, wholesalers, merchandisers and 'cash and carry' warehouses.

CASE ANALYSIS

A main negative to be overcome

The threat of negative PR and trade communications from main competitor.

CASE NARRATIVE

Alternative routes to market existed but there was significant variability of quality and coverage and FGD had had very few dealings with these alternatives.

Patel wholesalers covered 70% of the market but were weak in the North West.

'Cash and carry' warehouses were nationwide but would only do business on their terms and gave no guarantees of sales volumes and were generally not prepared to be loyal to suppliers.

Merchandising service companies were also servicing the market – the best being Rhonda mobile merchandising, which was nationwide and had the potential for 10% of national sales.

Marketing assessed that:

The total market for FGD was currently worth £500m in value.

FGD was the market leader with a share of 25% with a growth forecast to 26%.

This performance was good compared with the rest of the group – which was 18%.

Market growth was forecast to be low at 2%

CASE ANALYSIS

A main positive to be exploited
Alternative distributor – Patel wholesalers.

A main positive to be exploited
Alternative distributor – Rhonda mobile merchandising.

A main negative to be overcome
Low market growth at 2%.

Pivotal Question template

Qu

How can   [I/We/The Entity]   *The Family Grocers Division*

[Main action]   *combine the best of alternative distribution options*

in order to Overcome: and Exploit:

the loss of product availability from   *alternative third party*
ceasing direct deliveries   *distributors*

[Issue]   [Opportunity]

the threat of negative PR   *some reinvestment of the £15m cost*
from main competitor   *savings*

[Issue]   [Opportunity]

the need to save £15m costs
over three years

[Issue]   [Opportunity]

the loss of in-store control

[Issue]   [Opportunity]

slow market growth

[Issue]   [Opportunity]

                     annual volume to grow by 8% to 6.5m cases
                     PBT to grow by 10% to £22m

To achieve   [Pre-set objectives]   *£15m cost savings*

                     to continue to be the brand leader in all its market segments

And/or   [Aim]

Qu   *How can we combine the strengths of the alternative distribution options to retain our 80% market coverage and current in-store control, counter the threat of negative PR whilst exploiting our cost savings, ensure that we meet our pre-set objectives and achieve our aim to continue to be the brand leader in all market segments?*

YOUR PROJECT

From your setting bring forward your entity, aim and any pre-set objectives.

Here you have the opportunity to continue your project. Just follow the instructions

Your entity

Your aim

Your pre-set objectives

Review all the factors in your project and identify the main negative factors that will impede your progress towards your aim and that must be overcome.

Your negative factors that must be overcome
_____
_____
_____
_____
_____
_____
_____
_____
_____
_____
_____
_____
_____
_____
_____
_____
_____
_____
_____
_____
_____
_____
_____
_____
_____
_____
_____
_____
_____

Review all the factors in your project and identify the main positive factors that you can exploit in order to progress towards your aim.

Your positive opportunities to be exploited

YOUR PROJECT

Refer back to your causal chain diagram and clarify your main action.

Don't forget, your main action is an action at the strategic level that will lead to your aim. It contains no details but it must communicate strongly the direction you are going to take.

Your main action

_____

_____

_____

_____

_____

_____

_____

_____

_____

_____

_____

_____

_____

_____

_____

_____

_____

_____

Use the template opposite and build (from the bottom up) your first attempt at your pivotal question. You will need a number of attempts before you get it right – be patient!

When you have completed the template opposite, phrase your question as shown at the bottom of page 78.

Pivotal Question template

Qu

How can [I/We/The Entity]

[Main action]

in order to Overcome: and Exploit:

[Issue] [Opportunity]

[Issue] [Opportunity]

[Issue] [Opportunity]

[Issue] [Opportunity]

[Issue] [Opportunity]

To achieve [Pre-set objectives]

And/or [Aim]

'...he does this every time he gets something right, but thankfully it's a rare event!'

> If we can really understand the problem, the answer
> will come out of it, because the answer is not separate
> from the problem
>
> **Jiddu Krishnamurti**

CHAPTER 5

FINDING THE RIGHT ANSWER

In the last chapter I explored the importance of the pivotal question. In principle, the pivotal question or '**Qu**' in the SCQuARE mnemonic is a single question that all issues and facts turn upon, and when answered it shows you the best direction towards the achievement of your stretching aim.

Although the pivotal question shows you (or signifies) the best direction, it does no more than 'suggest' what you are going to do as you proceed in that direction. Knowing what you are going to do as a high-level strategy becomes clear as you find the answer to the question. In this chapter, I will describe how we find this answer – the '**A**' in the SCQuARE mnemonic.

What does an Answer look like?

Imagine you asked me a question – "*Ross, what do I have to do to achieve my aim?*" I could give you an answer that bears little relationship to the question. In this case you reject the answer immediately. Then, I may give you an answer that only addresses a part of the question. Again you reject this but you are now frustrated. So, I give you a full but long-winded answer that contains too much detail and the core message of the answer is lost in the excess. Again, you reject this answer. Finally, I give you an answer that forces you to pay attention – in fact it compels you to believe that it is right. Not only is it compelling, it has a number of benefits to you and it is so clear and succinct that there is no doubt or possibility of misunderstanding. Now, you accept the answer.

You now have the structure of the right answer. First, it compels you to believe that it is right. Secondly, it has clear benefits. Thirdly, it clearly states 'what' you have to do in a very succinct manner – in effect, a high-level strategy. Finally, the answer is without ambiguity or any possibility of alternative interpretations.

I mentioned that the answer is a high-level strategy. What I mean by this is that the answer is a summary of 'what' you have to do and at this stage it contains no detail of 'how' or 'why'. Just as the pivotal question is the whole analysis focused into a question, the answer is the whole solution focused by an answer.

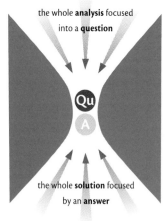

the whole **analysis** focused into a **question**

Qu

A

the whole **solution** focused by an **answer**

As the diagram shows, the answer will later expand to become the details of the 'how' and 'why' of the solution – that is the subject of the next chapter when we explore and develop the final parts '**R**' and '**E**' of the SCQuARE mnemonic.

For example, if I refer back to the Family Grocers Division case study, part of the answer to the pivotal question for John (see later) is to 'provide focused support promotional campaigns'. This is a high-level 'what' which will be fully developed and detailed later by the 'how' and 'why'.

In this example, I say that 'provide focused support promotional campaigns' is part of the answer. What do I mean by part? Clearly, 'provide focused support promotional campaigns' satisfies the criteria that it is an 'answer' – as you will see later in the case, it is compelling and believable, it has benefits, it is succinct and it cannot be misunderstood. And it is a high-level strategy that will lead towards the aim.

But in itself it will not achieve the aim and the 'whole' answer is a number of these high-level strategies that combine together. The compulsion and the ability to create immediate belief is the synergy of the parts – the individual strategies – that come together to form the whole.

Now that you know what an answer looks like, I can start to describe the process you use to develop an answer. This process is very systematic and it ensures that the answer is firmly connected with the pivotal question.

Developing the Answer; by cross referencing the question

The first step is to 'unravel' the pivotal question. This is simply done by using the information on the pivotal question template. You will recall that the pivotal question was developed by focusing on a conceptual structure:

'How can I take '**a main action**' to '**overcome any issues**'

and '**exploit any opportunities**' so that I will meet my

'**pre-set objectives**' and I will achieve my '**stated aim**'?

Systematically, I created the pivotal question by filling in the gaps and the pivotal question template helped me to do this.

On numerous occasions I have mentioned that the pivotal question has to 'show' or 'signify' the direction and this is contained in 'the main action'. For example, in the Family Grocers Division case study the main action is to 'combine the best of alternative distribution options'.

Strategy Matrix template		
The Entity		
The Aim		
Pre-set Objectives		
Main Action		
Changes and/or Complications		
ISSUE	0	
ISSUE	0	
ISSUE	0	
ISSUE	0	
Unexploited Opportunities		
OPPORTUNITY	0	
OPPORTUNITY	0	
OPPORTUNITY	0	
OPPORTUNITY	0	
Strategies for Evaluation	strategy 1	strategy 2

My main task is to develop an answer – in effect, a combination of a number of high-level strategies – that takes this main action and converts it into what I have to do. Importantly, what I have to do also has to 'overcome any issues' and 'exploit any opportunities' so that I will meet my 'pre-set objectives' and I will achieve my 'stated aim'. At the risk of labouring the point – the question and the answer are connected not just by actions you need to take but by all of the setting and consequence analysis that you have done to this stage, this being all brought together by the systematic process of developing the pivotal question.

You can work on the answer and check it by using the strategy matrix, part of which is shown alongside. Most of this information is contained on the pivotal question template. For the sake of illustration, this matrix contains a single strategy – strategy 1, which you can find at the bottom of the matrix. (The full matrix is at the end of this chapter.)

In principle, this matrix says that a strategy has to be evaluated in order to see whether the strategy meets the criteria of the pivotal question. For example, will strategy 1 exploit my opportunities and meet the changes and/

or complications and be a part of my main action? If this is the case, then this strategy will be part of my answer which will lead to me meeting any pre-set objectives and my aim. As you will see later, the evaluation is a simple numbering system.

Let me show you an example of this strategy matrix working. I will use one of the strategies in the Family Grocers Division case study and this is shown opposite.

The entity and aim, pre-set objectives and the main actions are contained on the pivotal question template and are simply transferred onto the strategy matrix (not shown in this example). As we know, the main action is 'combine the best of alternative distribution options'. From the pivotal question template I have listed the changes and complications and the opportunities – against these I have allocated a number between 0 (having no impact) and 5 (having a high impact).

For the purpose of this example and book I wish to keep the evaluation of strategies as simple as possible, so I will focus just on the use of a 'raw' number e.g. a number 5. However, as you know, you can improve the evaluation of strategies by weighting the various factors. For example, 'the need to save

Strategy Matrix template	
THE ENTITY	
THE AIM	
PRE-SET OBJECTIVES	
MAIN ACTION	
CHANGES AND/OR COMPLICATIONS	
loss of product availability from ceasing direct deliveries	5
threat of negative PR from main competitor	0
need to save £15m costs	5
loss of in-store control	5
low market growth	0
UNEXPLOITED OPPORTUNITIES	
strength of alternative distribution channels	5
reinvestment of the £15m savings that should materialise	1
Strategies for Evaluation	Patel Wholesalers

£15 m costs' could be weighted more highly than 'loss of in-store control'. This would then greatly affect the factors in the evaluation, putting greater emphasis on 'the need to save £15 m costs'.

At the bottom you will see that I have a strategy for evaluation – this is shown by the shorthand of 'Patel wholesalers'. In full, this strategy will be to use the Patel wholesalers as part of a combined distribution plan because it has 70% coverage of the market.

As I read up the matrix it says that using the Patel wholesalers only partially exploits the potential savings of £15 m but significantly exploits the strength of an alternative distribution channel. This will mean I can save significant costs by ceasing direct deliveries. Unfortunately, using Patel will not counter any negative PR from my main competitor nor will they affect a low growth market. However, they do provide in-store control.

Clearly, this strategy is likely to be part of my answer – in itself it is compelling and believable, it certainly has benefits and it is clear and succinct without any possibility of misunderstanding. And it will lead towards my aim. (You will find this example more fully developed at the end of this chapter.)

Creating and selling the right strategies

Only in the simplest of cases will you find that you have a single strategy that is the answer to the pivotal question. Most times, you will have a number of strategies that combine into the answer. How do you create these strategies? The best way is to use a combination of your experience and your creativity and the first task is to create a list of possible strategies.

Focus on the main action that you have stated on the pivotal question template. This main action is broken down into manageable parts. For example, John in the Family Grocers Division case study has to 'combine the best of alternative distribution options'. He's an experienced man and he would make a list of all possible distribution channels and analyse their strengths and weaknesses in relation to his aim. Some he would reject immediately because they are not applicable, whilst others would be shortlisted for further consideration.

Whilst John is doing this he would also be aware of the changes, complications and opportunities that his analysis has identified to date. To meet these criteria, John will most certainly have to support any distribution options he plans to use – this support could be advertising and/or merchandising. In effect, John builds up a series of strategies in readiness for the final evaluation on the strategy matrix.

In time, you will have a shortlist of possible strategies. Now, you need to do your first reduction and select the strong and discard the weak. Those most important to you will be those strategies that directly address any changes that created your situation in the first instance and/or those strategies that utilise any major opportunities and release synergetic benefits.

w h o o o

Eventually you will arrive at a point where you have a reduced list of strategies that you know will be

'When my boss said I was a bird brain, I'm sure he meant I was a high-flier.'

relevant. Using the strategy matrix, place these strategies on the bottom row, as a whole collection, and then evaluate, giving a number for each – just like in the example I gave earlier.

Some strategies will be good for (say) coping with the changes. Others may be good for keeping a complication under control. Whilst others may be good for releasing the potential of opportunities. You are searching for the combination of strategies that complete the matrix effectively – each strategy supporting each other strategy until an effective whole is created. This 'whole' is your answer.

Now, use the tests. Is your answer compelling? Is there any doubt or potential disbelief that it will lead to the main aim? Does it have clear and desirable benefits? Is it succinct and clear? Is there any possibility of misunderstanding? Don't forget you will not have the complete answer yet – you need to create the detailed action plan (see next chapter) before you have a fully worked out and robust answer.

Problems you might find

Finding the right answer is not always clear-cut. There are five main problems that you should be aware of.

First, let the pivotal question 'direct' you to the answer and it will do this if the pivotal question is well defined. If you are NOT making good progress with finding your answer, then it could be that the pivotal question needs to be checked again to make certain that it 'shows' the answer. Don't forget, just as defining the pivotal question is iterative, so is finding the answer – the question and the answer are always connected and it takes time to see this connection in its true light.

Secondly, many 'answers' sound brilliant when they first emerge but then they go on to fail in practice. Generally, this happens when all of the issues in the pivotal question have not been addressed fully.

Thirdly, as you endeavour to answer the question you will find that new factors begin to emerge. In the main, these new factors will be new complications and they will need to be taken into account and dealt with.

For example, imagine a marketing manager who has progressed well with the framing of a question that contains the complication that a major competitor always spends more on advertising than the marketing manager can afford. This leads the manager to consider strategy A as part of the answer. But then the manager considers an important 'what if' scenario – 'what happens if the competitor introduces web promotion as well as above-the-line advertising?' Now, the manager has a new complication which will have to be dealt with.

Fourthly, when you start to answer the question you will find that you could develop too many strategies! From a creativity standpoint this is good, but it reminds me to point out a basic reflection on developing strategy and tactics – you have to decide what you are NOT going to do! One of the beauties of using the strategy matrix is that it quickly shows you which strategies to discard.

Finally, almost as a contradiction to the point I have just raised, is the point of 'familiarity' – things you have done in the past are things you will do in the future. Some people call these 'tried and trusted' ways, whilst others will call these same ways 'unimaginative'. Even at the risk of creating more possible answers to your question, you still must focus upon really creative answers because these could be the only ones that are capable of being the direction towards your stretching aim.

Summary

The pivotal question is the whole analysis focused into a question. The answer to this question is the whole solution focused by this answer. The question and answer are always connected and together – this is the core of the SCQuARE process.

The answer is, in the general case, a combination of high-level strategies that create a compelling and believable whole. These combined strategies contain very little detail but they do give a very clear and succinct meaning to what you are going to do.

As you can see in this chapter, finding the right answer is a logical and analytical process. This then becomes the springboard for creativity around the detailed execution of your strategies. This process can be further enhanced by the use of another SCQUARE International technique and toolkit called BREAKER. BREAKER introduces methods of generating more inspiring and game changing ideas, it creates the stimulus for people to be more creative and imaginative around their strategies. BREAKER is described in chapter nine, page 169 onwards.

Case study

I'll now update the case study for the answer. After shortlisting a number of strategies John believes that there are four strategies in combination that will form his answer.

As you can see overleaf, John has completed his strategy matrix.

From his pivotal question template John has filled in (from the top) the entity, the aim, the pre-set objectives and the main action. Whatever combined strategies John decides to use, he knows that these aims, objectives and actions are paramount and should feature in his evaluation.

Again, from the pivotal question template John has filled in (down the left-hand side) all the changes, complications and the opportunities.

At the bottom John has filled in his shorthand strategies. From the left, he has filled in two distributors who will form the foundation of the new distribution system when direct deliveries cease – together these two distributors will create the 80% market coverage that is required, with good in-store control, and each will help to counter weaknesses in the other.

You will recall from earlier parts of the case study that Patel was a wholesaler that covered 70% of the market and, clearly, Patel was the mainstay of any new distribution approach.

To support this new nationwide distribution it would be necessary to use the services of Rhonda merchandising who would ensure that shelves were fully

Strategy Matrix

The Entity				
Family Grocers Division				

Aims	Patel Wholesalers	Rhonda Merchandising	Support promotions	Competitive advertising
to continue to be the brand leader in all its market segments	4	3	4	4

Pre-set Objectives				
annual volumes to grow by 8% to 6.5m cases	2	2	3	4
profit before tax to grow by 10% to £22m	2	2	2	3
£15m cost savings	2	2	2	2

Main Action				
combine the strengths of alternative distribution options				

Changes/Complications				
loss of product availability from ceasing direct deliveries	5	5	5	0
threat of negative PR from main competitor	0	0	1	5
the need to save £15m costs	5	5	4	0
loss of in-store control	5	5	3	0
low market growth	0	2	4	1

Unexploited opportunities				
the strength of alternative distribution channels	5	5	0	0
reinvestment of the £15m savings that should materialise	1	1	5	5

Strategies for evaluation	Patel Wholesalers	Rhonda Merchandising	Support promotions	Competitive advertising

stocked with available products throughout the distribution channels as well as provide the additional 10% market coverage.

John knows that these new distributors will need to be supported by promotional campaigns and incentive schemes. Finally, John knows that he will have to mount an advertising campaign to offset any negative promotions of the main competitor, Walkers. To fund these campaigns John will need to use some of the projected savings of £15 m. John's pivotal question was:

How can we combine the strengths of the alternative distribution options to retain our 80% market coverage and current in-store control, counter the threat of negative PR whilst exploiting our cost savings, ensure that we meet our pre-set objectives and achieve our aim to continue to be the brand leader in all market segments?

John's answer is (subject to revision by later action plans):

We can meet our pre-set objectives and our aim if we retain our 80% market coverage by combining the coverage of Patel and Rhonda and reinvest some of the savings to provide focused distributor support, promotional campaigns and counter the threat of Walker's negative advertising with our own positive trade and distributor's campaign.

YOUR PROJECT

From your experience and from using creativity techniques, create a long-list of individual strategies that could lead to the achievement of your aim.

Here you have the opportunity to continue your project.
Just follow the instructions

_____

Your aim

_____

Individual strategies

_____

Shortlist your strategies into an overall strategy.

Overall combined strategies

Is your overall strategy:

Compelling and believable?

Does it have clear benefits?

Does it state 'what'?

Is it clear and succinct?

Insert your overall combined strategies. From your pivotal question template fill in the spaces. Using a score between 0 and 5 evaluate each strategy.

Strategy Matrix template

The Entity			
Aim			
Pre-set Objectives			
Main Action			
Changes/Complications			
Unexploited opportunities			
Strategies for evaluation			

Your Pivotal Question was:

Qu

Your Answer is (subject to revision by later action plans):

A

RE

'...could we just quickly revisit the Pivotal Question
again? ... or maybe take one more turn around the
Causal chain?'

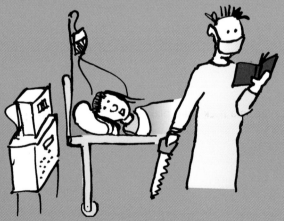

CHAPTER 6

MAKING THE ANSWER WORK

You may recall the funnel diagram on page 86. This diagram represented how the analysis, based on the setting and consequences, became 'concentrated' into a question. You then answered this question – this answer being a 'concentrated' solution, which then expanded into the whole solution.

I am now at the point where I can describe how the answer – a combination of high-level strategies – is turned into detailed plans that describe this whole solution. In effect, making the answer work. This is the '**RE**' of the SCQuARE mnemonic.

Creating a rock-solid plan

As I have just mentioned, an answer is a combination of high-level strategies. You will recall from the Family Grocers Division case study that these high-level strategies have no detail. For example, part of John's answer was to '**use Patel wholesalers and Rhonda merchandisers**'.

Imagine that you are my boss and I said to you *'to achieve my aim I'm going to use Patel wholesalers and Rhonda merchandisers'*. What is the question you will now ask? You will ask *'Ross, how are you going to do that?'* So, I probably give a reply containing a 'big idea' or something that I know will create interest. Probably, at some point, you will also ask *'good idea, why are you convinced it will work?'* At this point, I expand on why it will work and you nod that you are also convinced – or at least persuaded to listen to the whole plan.

The two questions 'how' and 'why' are the two questions that turn an answer into a plan. Even more importantly, the two questions have turned the plan into a persuasive case.

MY PLAN

'. . . bring on the Spanish Inquisition!'

Every time I ask a series of questions with 'how' in them, I turn the answer into a plan. And then, every time I ask a series of questions with 'why' in them, I turn it into a convincing and persuasive plan.

In the SCQuARE mnemonic the 'how' questions are represented by the '**R**', meaning **recommendations** and the 'why' questions are represented by the '**E**', meaning **evidence**. In effect, I make a series of strong recommendations and I back each of these recommendations up with convincing and persuasive evidence.

Turning an Answer into an action plan

So, I start with an answer that contains no details but describes 'what' I am going to do. For example, in the case study, part of John's overall answer was to '**use Patel wholesalers and Rhonda merchandisers**', so this is John's start point.

STEP 1

My first step in creating a plan is to define the main idea that gives the plan its focus and persuasive power – the 'big idea' as it were. This main idea could be an activity, a decision, a process and so on. For example, John could create the main idea of '**sign a rolling three-year agreement with Patel and Rhonda that guarantees our minimum volumes and commits Patel and Rhonda to non-competitive trading**'. Clearly, although this is a 'big idea' John would be keen to seek agreement, bearing in mind that the Patel wholesalers cover 70% of the market and Rhonda have the potential to cover 10% of the market and therefore both distributors are critical to the achievement of John's aim.

Now, to ensure it is persuasive, I have to back up this main idea with a compelling reason or strong evidence that the idea will work.

For example, John knows that a rolling three-year agreement based on virtually exclusive volumes with the Family Grocers Division, the market leader, is a very attractive proposal to Patel wholesalers and Rhonda merchandisers because it stabilises their sales and market position.

Let me put this example into conversational mode to demonstrate how the 'how' and 'why' work to create a really powerful start to the action plan.

> **HOW?**
>
> for every strategy ask 'what is my main idea?
>
> this creates focus and persuasion
>
> **WHY?**
>
> for every main idea give a compelling reason or strong evidence

Imagine you are John's boss and John says to you:

'*To achieve my aim I'm going to use Patel wholesalers and Rhonda merchandisers.*'

In response, you say:

'*John, how are you going to do this?*'

John answers:

'I'm going to sign a rolling three-year agreement with both of them that guarantees our minimum volumes and commits them to non-competitive trading.'

You say:

'Why will they do this?'

John replies:

'It's a very attractive proposal for Patel and Rhonda because it gives virtually exclusive volumes, it stabilises their sales and market position and at the same time, it stabilises our sales at the level we need.'

I think you can see from this conversation how powerful a start we now have for turning a strategy into a convincing and persuasive plan.

I am purposefully using the conversational mode. As a matter of practice when you are at this stage and detailing your plans, always keep asking questions and providing answers as though you were in conversation with your boss. This will ensure that you get into the necessary detail. Importantly, as you will see in the next chapter, using the conversational mode creates added power to the persuasion – and this leads to a YES.

Now that I have my main idea I can continue to use the 'how' and 'why' questions to put more detail into the plan.

STEP 2

The second step is to create a short series of linked support ideas that will back up the main idea. Again, these support ideas could be activities, decisions, processes or whatever, depending upon the nature of the plan.

> **HOW?**
>
> **for every main idea ask 'how will I back this up'?**
>
> **this creates a list of support ideas**
>
> **WHY?**
>
> **for every support idea give a compelling reason or strong evidence**

Again, the process is to ask 'how' and 'why'. For example, for John's main idea, 'sign a rolling three-year agreement with Patel and Rhonda that guarantees our minimum volumes and commits Patel and Rhonda to non-competitive trading', John asks himself 'how am I going to back this up?' Thinking this through John knows that he will have to provide a 'package' of incentives that will build up the confidence of Patel and Rhonda that the three-year rolling agreement is the right way to go. He creates a list of three support ideas:

- Reduce the standard sale margin for sales below a set limit.
- Introduce a high-value volume discount scheme.
- Introduce a support promotions and sales incentive scheme.

John knows that Patel and Rhonda will be motivated by volume of sales and overall profit. Clearly, a non-competitive trading agreement with John's business, the market leader, is very attractive as it almost guarantees the volumes that will excite Patel and Rhonda.

To create the right motivation for Patel and Rhonda, John wants to reduce the standard margin but offset this with a high-value volume discount scheme and support this with various promotions and sales force incentives.

Finally, John wants to give added power to this plan by asking the question 'why'. His thinking is clear. Patel and Rhonda will commit to this plan because they will achieve a much higher volume of guaranteed sales at a greater overall profit. And with all the promotional support and sales force support they will be greatly motivated to do very well.

Let me now put this into conversational mode with you as John's boss (from the start):

John says:

'To achieve my aim I'm going to use Patel wholesalers and Rhonda merchandisers.'

In response, you say:

'John, how are you going to do this?'

John answers:

'I'm going to sign a rolling three-year agreement with both of them that guarantees our minimum volumes and commits them to non-competitive trading.'

You say:

'Why will they do this?'

John replies:

'It's a very attractive proposal for Patel and Rhonda because it gives virtually exclusive volumes that stabilises their sales and market position and at the same time, it stabilises our sales at the level we need.'

You say:

'How will you make this work?'

John replies:

'I'm going to introduce a high-incentive sales volume scheme supported by focused promotions and sales force incentives.'

You say:

'Why will this work?'

John says:

'I'm going to reduce the standard margin and offset this with a high-value volume discount scheme that will significantly increase their overall profits as they hit the targets we need. Our support promotions will create very good motivation for Patel and Rhonda and in particular, their sales force will be highly rewarded for their success.'

'... on your specialist subject, "alternative distribution systems" you have 18 correct answers and no passes'

You say:

'Sounds good so far.'

John replies:

'Yes, it's a winning situation for us both. As they achieve more we achieve more – both volumes and overall profits. And, it ties them into a rolling three-year agreement that lays a good base for our new distribution system so we can achieve our aim.'

You say:

'How are you going to cope with Walker's negative campaign?'

John says:

'When I know their reaction, I'm going to introduce our trade advertising campaign designed to counter any of the potential damage they can create.'

You say:

'I like it. Get on with it.'

Sounds pretty convincing to me – what do you think? So, to summarise this section. For your answer you develop a main idea by asking 'how' and 'why'. You then go on and develop a list of support ideas by again asking 'how' and 'why'. The more you question, the more you get into the detail and the more convincing you make your plan.

Finally, you turn your plan into an imaginary conversation and you verbalise the overall flow of your case. As you follow this conversation you will see the strengths and weaknesses of your plan and your case. Each rehearsal strengthens the plan and makes it even more persuasive.

STEP 3

Most plans in a business or managerial situation use resources. There are three resources that are paramount – money, time and people. Therefore, step three of the plan is to put it into a resource context. For example, you may need to cost

> If HOW is the cost, then WHY is the benefit.
>
> If HOW is the action, then WHY is the reason

your plan in detail and/or look at investment costs and returns and so on. Your plan will almost certainly have a series of activities and these will need to be detailed with timings. Finally, all plans will use people or team resources and these will need to be allocated to the plan and HR control systems put in place.

The pre-emptive questions

The final part of your planning process is to check your plan with pre-emptive questions. These questions will make your plan stronger by ensuring that some important issues are not overlooked. It is useful to think of these pre-emptive questions as potential questions that your boss could ask. Every plan you put together will have unique issues and information and therefore unique pre-emptive questions. However, there are certain pre-emptive questions that must be covered.

I can paint a good picture of these pre-emptive questions by looking at the basic practices of project planning – in my 'tour' below I will bring out the pre-emptive questions into highlighted summary boxes. Any of these pre-emptive questions could cause problems for you.

In overview, a project plan is generally defined by a start time and finish time, a set of objectives and a sequence of activities that will lead to these objectives. All these plans will have a set of resources, generally a person or a team of people, finance and certain physical resources such as materials and equipment. They also have certain standards of performance.

I'll build up a bit of detail. For example, a plan has an outcome represented by a set of objectives. These objectives have to be well defined and clear to all

> **Are your strategies clear and succinct?**
>
> **Are your objectives well defined and clear?**
>
> **Are your priorities well defined and clear?**

persons. In 'management-speak' these objectives are SMART – Specific, Measurable, Achievable, Realistic and Timed. Even though all objectives should be 'smart', not all objectives are equally important, so you have different priorities between objectives.

If you have different priorities between objectives then you have different priorities between any associated activities. In effect, the whole project plan is a priority management system generally represented by a network of critical events, critical dates and critical paths. Any errors or mismanagement of these events and times or on these paths, will lead to significant problems in the plan and its ability to achieve the objectives. More so, imagine what could happen if you were NOT to identify all the critical activities and timings.

> **Have you considered all the critical matters?**
>
> **What are the risks if problems arise?**
>
> **Have you identified all important matters?**

> **Do you have adequate resources for the job?**
>
> **Are your financial expectations realistic?**
>
> **Will your plan meet investment and cash objectives?**

All plans have to cope with constraints. For example, time for all activities may be constrained if the finish time is to be met.

Or financial resources are likely to be constrained and if a budget were to overrun, this could jeopardise the whole project. These constraints may be many and varied but they all operate in the same way – if the constraint is not met it could develop into a significant limiting factor that puts the whole project at risk.

All plans use different types of resources controlled by budgets. For example, you are allocated a certain amount of (say) space, raw materials, equipment and so on. In particular you are allocated money and this money is controlled by an investment plan that expects certain returns to justify the

> **Have you identified all important constraints?**
>
> **Could a constraint become a limiting factor?**
>
> **Could a constraint become a down-size risk?**

investment. As the plan unfolds, a set of financial budgets will control other factors such as sales, margins, costs, profits and cash.

> **Do you have the right team and skills?**
>
> **Is your team committed to the objectives?**
>
> **Have you considered all important stakeholders?**

When you explore team aspects of a plan you have to consider the team leader and the people in the team – their roles, skills and other qualities that they bring. These team members will need to be monitored for their performance and the quality of their work. This means standards and a performance management process.

Surrounding all, you have a team environment, generally made up of different personal goals, expectations and behavioural factors such as team motivation, commitment or positive/negative acceptance and so on.

Even though they are not directly within a team you also have to consider any important stakeholders in the plan. For example, your boss, your boss's boss, your customers and suppliers and so on.

For a plan to be successful you will need to consider very carefully how you will keep everyone informed, properly involved and up to date. Particularly, all those people who are affected by any changes that your plan can bring – you have to manage all the potential resistance that could emerge. So involvement and communication become critical management tasks and you need to plan for these.

Finally, as you proceed through your plan not everything will go according to the plan. You will meet unexpected problems. You may have to find new ways of doing things or new directions for achieving the same end points and so on. In effect, your plan evolves as it proceeds and you are looking ahead predicting threats to the plan and creating contingency plans to stay on-track.

> Do you have a communication plan?
>
> What are your plans for managing change?
>
> What are your plans for involving all affected?

It is useful to see how these pre-emptive questions work. Whilst John is asking 'how' and 'why' and detailing his plan, he has these pre-emptive questions in his mind.

For example, when he is considering the promotional schemes he is aware of

> What problems can you foresee at this stage?
>
> Are there matters ahead that are highly critical?
>
> What contingency plans have you considered?

the critical activities that will be involved, and in particular the time of putting in place a successful scheme. He foresees a potentially difficult question from his boss '*John, what happens to your projected returns if it takes six months to put a successful promotional scheme in place?*' John reviews this point in detail and decides to reduce this risk by a simpler scheme.

111

Summary

The pivotal question focuses the whole analysis into a single question. The answer to this question focuses the whole of the solution. To give the detail of this solution and to start to build a convincing and persuasive case you use the two questions 'how' and 'why'.

For each high-level strategy in turn, you ask 'how am I going to do this?' and the answer is a main idea or a 'big idea' that will bring the results you seek, and act as a powerful persuader. You ask 'why' in order to give your main idea a compelling reason or strong evidence for its likely success.

You continue the process of asking the 'how' and 'why' questions and develop a list of support ideas that give extra depth to the main idea. Again, every support idea has a compelling reason or strong evidence. To develop the flow of ideas and to check their persuasion, you create an imaginary conversation that covers all the ideas.

Finally, you detail the financial aspects, the timings and the people resources that are required for the plan. As a final check you review the whole of your plan with certain pre-emptive questions – these ensure that any potentially difficult matters that could arise later (say) during presentation are handled at this stage.

Back to the Family Grocers Division case study.

HOW CAN JOHN GET EVERYONE ON THE SAME PAGE?

Now that John has his answer he considers his main idea that will satisfy the answer. As highlighted in the text of this chapter his main idea is to sign a three-year agreement with Patel and Rhonda.

His support ideas are: a mainly self-funding volume incentive scheme supported by promotions and sales team incentives. To cope with the threat of negative advertising from Walkers, the main competitor, he plans his own counter advertising campaign once he knows their position.

He considers his resource context and develops his cost plan (see **RE** form overleaf). His total costs are £2m over the three-year period partly funded by using some of the £15m savings, but he is hopeful that the increase in volumes will make the whole plan highly productive.

His forecasts for the plan once in full operation are strong and positive and certainly meet the pre-set objectives and the aim. He plans to start the scheme in readiness for the new financial year and is happy that he has the personnel to implement the scheme.

He checked his plans with some pre-emptive questions and tackled a couple of potential problems that emerged.

His completed '**RE**' form is overleaf.

Recommendations & Evidence

SUMMARISED ANSWER Develop new channels supported with focused promotions

Main idea

HOW	WHY
Sign a rolling three year agreement with Patel and Rhonda that guarantees our minimum volumes and commits Patel and Rhonda to non-competitive trading	It gives virtually exclusive volumes that stabilise their sales and market position

Support Ideas

HOW 1	WHY 1
Reduce the standard sale margin for sales below a set limit	This creates a financial opportunity to introduce a high value incentive scheme

HOW 2	WHY 2
Introduce a high value volume discount scheme for sales above a set limit and set clear targets for these sales	This will increase Patel's and Rhonda's volume sales and overall profits from the agreement

HOW 3	WHY 3
Introduce a joint funded support promotional campaign and introduce a sales team incentive scheme for Patel and Rhonda	This creates motivation and loyalty and ensures that Patel's and Rhonda's sales teams will achieve their high volume targets

HOW 4	WHY 4
Introduce a trade advertising campaign designed to counter any negative trade campaign by Walkers, the main competitor	Essential to counter any competitor campaigns and support Patel and Rhonda in their new sales efforts under the new agreements

HOW 5	WHY 5

Resource context

Finance	WHY
The high value volume discount scheme will break even with additional incentive costs of £1m over three years and all other promotional and advertising costs will total £1m over three years. A total of £2m over three years	Over 3 years Patel's case sales will be 5,000, 5,500 and 6,500 and Rhonda's sales will be 2,000, 2,500 and 3,000
	Sales at this level achieve market share of 26% in year 1 and 27% and 28% in years 2 and 3.
	Profits will be £22m in year 1 and £25m and £28m in years 2 and 3

Timings	WHY
Start of our financial year	This co-ordinates financial year for all parties

Responsibility	WHY
Trade marketing	They have the resources and expertise available

YOUR PROJECT

Bring your answer forward and keep it uppermost in your workings.

Here you have the opportunity to continue your project.

Just follow the instructions.

Your answer here

Your main idea

How

Why

Your support ideas

How

Why

Your support ideas continued

How

_____

_____

_____

_____

Why

_____

_____

_____

_____

How

_____

_____

_____

_____

Why

_____

_____

_____

_____

How

_____

_____

_____

_____

Why

_____

_____

_____

_____

Consider your resource context.

Finance
_____
_____
_____
_____
_____

Consider your pre-emptive questions.
Use this checklist:

Timings
_____
_____
_____

Are your strategies clear and succinct?

Are your objectives well defined and clear?

Responsibility
_____

Are your priorities well defined and clear?

Have you considered all the critical matters?

What are the risks if problems arise?

Have you identified all important matters?

Have you identified all important constraints?

Pre-emptive questions
_____

Could a constraint become a limiting factor?

Could a constraint become a down-size risk?
_____

Do you have adequate resources for the job?
_____

Are your financial expectations realistic?
_____

Will you meet investment and cash objectives?
_____

Do you have the right team and skills?
_____

Is your team committed to the objectives?
_____

Have you considered all important stakeholders?
_____

Do you have a communication plan?
_____

What are your plans for managing change?
_____

What are your plans for involving all affected?
_____

What problems can you foresee at this stage?
_____

Are there matters ahead that are highly critical?

Rehearse your conversation and check that you have covered all matters and that your ideas flow well. Pay particular attention to the persuasive power of your conversation. You may wish to use your boss as your imaginary conversational partner.

Complete your project by using the 'RE' form opposite.

Your conversation

_____
_____
_____
_____
_____
_____
_____
_____
_____
_____
_____
_____
_____
_____
_____
_____
_____
_____
_____
_____
_____
_____
_____
_____
_____
_____
_____
_____
_____
_____

YOUR PROJECT

Recommendations & Evidence template

SUMMARISED ANSWER	Develop new channels supported with focused promotions

Main idea	
HOW	WHY

Support Ideas

HOW 1	WHY 1
HOW 2	WHY 2
HOW 3	WHY 3
HOW 4	WHY 4
HOW 5	WHY 5

Resource context	
Finance	WHY
Timings	WHY
Responsibility	WHY

story

'..and the case for the defence, m'Lud, is now available on Amazon and in all good bookshops!'

CHAPTER 7

TELLING A POWERFUL STORY

I have now completed the SCQuARE mnemonic. Throughout the book we have been thinking and reflecting. When we considered the '**S**' and '**C**' we were analysing. With the '**Qu**' and '**A**' we started to synthesise and became creative looking for a solution. Finally we made it all work with the '**RE**'.

Now I have the final task – to tell a powerful story that will get everyone on the same page. This task is not about thinking *per se*, it is about conviction and persuasion and that is why, in the previous chapter, I introduced the idea of holding an imaginary conversation about 'how' and 'why'.

What is a powerful story?

The best idea in the world is useless if you can't sell the idea. You may have the best ideas, plans and strategies but if your boss doesn't buy into them then they are all to no avail.

The best ideas become even better ideas once you have persuaded others and you can only persuade and sell if you have a powerful story that is compelling and thorough. But a powerful story is not a complicated story nor is it a long story. On the contrary, a powerful story is simple and concise and it follows a set plan that is designed to convince and persuade.

Let me give an example that is as far away from business as possible. Recently, I was having lunch with a famous film script writer and as it happens, a great story teller and writer of thrillers. Over lunch I mentioned my ideas about telling powerful business stories. To my surprise he completely agreed and said that he had similar ideas. He then went on to explain the 'formula' for all his powerful stories in his thriller films.

His take on the 'formula' was very illuminating. Imagine a thriller film taking about 110 minutes – apparently, the standard length and long enough to make the viewer satisfied and wanting more, but short enough to ensure maximum attention.

At exactly 10 minutes into the film there will be a very exciting incident – the sort of incident that makes you sit on the edge of your seat. At 30 minutes, there is a 'heroic incident' of some sort that defines the leading character and changes the whole direction of the film. For the next 60 minutes, a series of incidents build up, with each one of increasing strength and frequency. Following these incidents, at 98 minutes, the hero reaches an insurmountable problem which requires tremendous inner strength to solve and at 110 minutes this problem is finally solved.

'Does he really have to do that ten minutes into every meeting!'

Actually, I wish he had not told me this because every time

I go to a see a thriller film now, I always look at my watch – especially at 10 minutes! But the point is made. Powerful stories are not created by accident, they are produced by careful design and craft. You can translate the script writer's 'formula' into a typical business situation.

A good business story should be long enough to give the right substance but short enough to maintain interest. Very early on you have to create real interest by highlighting the essential 'problem'. This 'story' is then developed and eventually (at the imaginary 98th minute) the 'problem' has to be solved otherwise a business disaster follows. You step in with all the solutions – (phew, the hero has arrived!) – and your boss says YES!

More seriously, telling a powerful business story does have a 'formula' and that is what I now want to develop.

Using a storyboard to check sequence and emphasis

The foundation of a powerful story is a storyboard directly linked to your thinking. It shows the full extent of the story you are going to tell. Importantly, the story is structured by succinct headlines – these headlines being the powerful conclusions of all your work. Under each headline there are no more than three major points.

Imagine a presentation slide as shown in the diagram but the same ideas I will describe apply to verbalising a story in a conversation (as I did in the last chapter), or any other medium. To make this slide very powerful I have to have a good headline – the sort of thing that makes the audience sit on the edge of their seats! I can then make a maximum of three key points that gives the headline its substance.

Let me give you an example of this concept. You will remember in chapter two that I mentioned about giving a positive interpretation to your findings.

Actually, what we were doing at that point was creating the possible headlines we would use in telling the powerful story.

In the Family Grocers Division case study we found out that the division was in fact the star performer of the Group. And, this story could be told very powerfully and very simply as you can see in this slide. Later, I will develop this story in detail.

HEADLINE

Point 1

Point 2

Point 3

This concept of the headline supported by no more than three key points is the basic 'building block' of the story. The total length of the story is determined by the project – it may be six or sixty 'building blocks'. In principle each 'building block' will take no more than one or two minutes to explain.

FGD IS THE GROUP'S STAR PERFROMER

We lead a large mature market

Nationwide availability

Sales growth +8%

On page 126 you will see that I have translated these ideas into a full storyboard, using as an example, twelve slides – but the principles apply to any length of storyboard.

I would like to make two important points. First, if you were to look at this story in overview you would find that the headlines tell the whole story in a powerful way – this is a real test of a good story. If there were no information other than just the headlines, is the story still told? If yes, then you have a very persuasive story. You'll see this point being made later in the case study.

Secondly, the storyboard follows the SCQuARE mnemonic. The number of slides per section may vary depending upon your story but I'll use a typical arrangement for my explanations.

The first slide is an '**S**' slide. It gives an agenda and shows the audience where you are going. It also contains a 'hook' that presents a dramatic benefit (more later).

You then have further '**S**' slides, showing the entity, aim and pre-set objectives, and the main points of the setting.

This is followed by slides on the '**C**' of the SCQuARE mnemonic. These slides make the key points of the changes, complications, opportunities and the consequences.

You then have slides showing the pivotal question and the answer. These are the '**Qu**' and '**A**' of the SCQuARE mnemonic.

These are followed by slides of recommendations and evidence or the '**RE**' of the mnemonic. The final '**RE**' slide is a summary and the key benefit of the whole story – the benefit that deserves a YES. And, if it deserves a YES, then ask for a YES!

Clearly, you can have variations of this theme. Your storyboard may be slightly shorter or longer. It may have four slides for a section rather than three and so on. All of these variations are fine.

Now that I have explained about the storyboard I can get into a little more detail.

You must sell the problem

In my example earlier, you the hero, stepped in at the '98th minute' and solved the problem for all. Well done and what a relief!

Actually, the reason why you were seen as the hero is not just because you solved the problem but because you also 'sold' the problem to everybody in the first place! Plainly – if you don't sell the problem, then you can't get everyone on the same page, so no one is going to buy your solution.

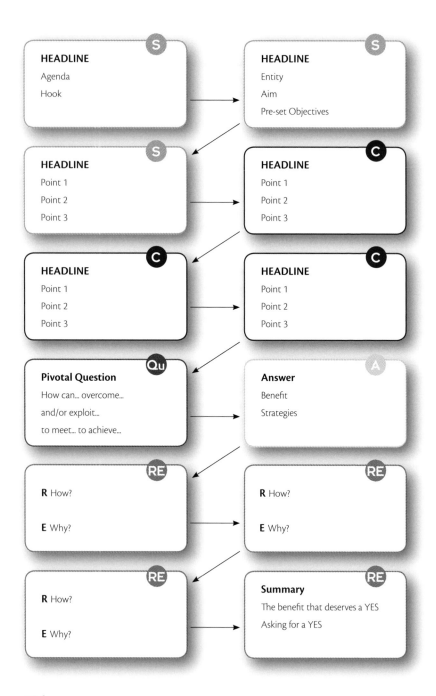

This observation is one of the reasons why SCQuARE has been so successful. It meticulously and convincingly builds the problem from first principles, so that by the time you give the answer to the pivotal question the problem is well and truly sold.

As the problem is built from first principles it is very important that you pay attention to three matters.

First, a person does not process lots of information, they process only the information that is required – anything more leads either to an overload or a disregard. The eminent psychologist George Miller writing in *Principia Cybernetica* in 1956 noted that:

> *'Humans can reliably distinguish, recognise or name*
> *no more than seven, plus or minus two values. More and*
> *finer distinctions cause confusion and unreliability.'*

This is the principal reason why the storyboard should be as short as possible, with each 'building block' having a headline and no more than three key points. The headline and the few key points are creating 'nuggets' of information in its simplest form such that it is clear and valid.

If for some reason your story is very complicated with lots of information, then you must simplify it by putting the data into categories and a hierarchy – for example, a hierarchy of seven categories and so on.

Secondly, a story needs to be presented inductively and not deductively. This sounds complicated but my points are simple.

When you are thinking deductively you are generally looking at data and drawing your conclusions on what you find. So, the sequence is 'data' followed by 'conclusion'.

When you are thinking inductively you generally have an overview (or conclusion) and you are looking for data to support it. So, the sequence is 'conclusion' followed by 'data'.

Now imagine these issues in your story. If you present deductively, that is 'data' first, you invite unwanted questions or allow your audience to jump to their own conclusion, which then means that you may have to change their mind. Worse, your audience does not know where you are going or what conclusion you are going to draw and this creates frustration.

The golden rule is to present your conclusion first, then back this up with the information. For example, the headline is acting as a conclusion, which is then backed up by three key points.

Finally, don't underestimate the importance of the headlines. A strong headline adds value and it engages an audience in your overall story. I made the point earlier that all headlines together make the story – even without all the backup points. You can see this working in the diagrams below; on the left-hand side are slides showing the typical convention of labels whereas the slides on the right show headlines. Which are better?

BACKGROUND	FIVE YEARS OF GROWTH
Point 1	Point 1
Point 2	Point 2
Point 3	Point 3

CASHFLOW	BREAK EVEN IN TWO YEARS
Point 1	Point 1
Point 2	Point 2
Point 3	Point 3

The golden rule is simple. Resist all urges to use labels and create a headline instead. As you are creating your headline keep asking yourself 'so what?' until you find a short headline that adds value and perspective to the maximum of three points you are making.

As I mentioned earlier, your basic headlines are the positive interpretations you created in your setting (chapter 2). Work and paraphrase these positive statements into punchy headlines with no more than six words.

Building the story

I would now like to follow the storyboard, bringing out key points as I build the story. You may wish to refer back to the overview diagram on page 126 but don't forget that the number of slides in any section will vary depending upon the story to be told.

The **first slide** contains a headline and two main points – the agenda and the 'hook'. The most important information on this slide is the 'hook' because it creates a sense of drama and it promises a benefit that you know the audience is seeking. For example, if your audience is seeking growth and profits then the 'hook', 'Seven sure ways to make money' sets up their expectations in a pithy and dramatic manner. The headline simply reflects the 'hook' (say) – 'More growth means more profits'.

The agenda is the overview of your story. It shows your audience where they are going and what you are going to cover and it firmly establishes the subject of your story. Keep your agenda short and sweet – you do not want to deal with any questions at this early stage.

> **HEADLINE**
>
> Agenda
>
> 'Hook'
>
> S

> **HEADLINE**
> Entity
> Aim
> Pre-set Objectve

The **second slide** gives an overview of the entity, aim and any important pre-set objectives. You will recall that the entity gives (amongst other things) the scope and time frame of your project, so this is very important orientation information that must be given. The aim sets out what you want to achieve – don't forget the aim has to be seen as a stretching achievement because a stretching achievement helps to persuade and will add power to your story. The headline will be based on the aim. For example (building on the previous example) the headline could be 'Growth up 10% – Profits up 15%' if the aim was (say) to find new business opportunities for increasing growth and profits.

Finally, you need to spell out any important pre-set objectives. It is best to give these in summarised form because it is likely that the audience is familiar with these and therefore too much information serves no purpose.

> **HEADLINE**
> Part 1
> Part 2
> Part 3

The **third slide** contains the 'meat' of your analysis of the setting. For example, in the Family Grocers Division case study the setting contained market data showing that the market was worth £500 m and the positive interpretation that John put on this was 'it is a large market with fragmented ownership'. John could create the headline 'Our market is large and fragmented' and then go on to make the points that give substance.

The important point to make about any slides in the setting is that they should always be factual, positive and non-controversial. The setting is always about creating positive agreement of the facts and about avoiding any difficult questions at this stage.

130

I use the idea of the 'nodding dogs' because at this stage you are looking for positive body language indicating agreement – imagine a nodding dog in the rear window of a car! Get your story right at this stage and you will see lots of nodding heads.

The **fourth, fifth** and **sixth** slides are about changes, complications and, in particular, about consequences. If there are any difficult issues to be dealt with in your story, then this is where they will be presented – so always be careful at this point.

These slides are about the matters or problems that your later propositions in the story are seeking to resolve and/or solve. So you are covering the main weaknesses and threats (the negatives to be overcome) and the opportunities (the positives to be exploited).

It is important to keep your causal chain analysis firmly in your mind. The root causes are the base line of your arguments – these are the things that are given and outside your control. If you can convince your audience of these root causes then you have generally made progress in your persuasion. In particular, the causal chain analysis leads naturally to the opportunities that you can exploit – so you are ending a potentially difficult part of your story on a positive, and with a sound indication of a solution.

> **HEADLINE**
> Point 1
> Point 2
> Point 3
>
> **C**

For example, John in the Family Grocers Division case study (see page 32) has 'economic uncertainty' and 'fragmented and mature market' as two of his root causes. In turn, economic uncertainty causes rising fuel and labour costs causing high costs of distribution. A fragmented and mature market means traditional channels of direct deliveries, leading to (again) high costs of distribution.

As John comes up the causal chain, these causes result in the decision to cease direct deliveries, which in turn exposes the high risk of loss of market share and profits. Although John's situation is difficult, he is using powerful logic in his analysis as he builds the 'problem' in his audience's mind. Don't forget, to sell the solution you must first sell the problem! And, as you will remember, John's solution is to combine the best of his available distribution options – if he sells the problem he will sell this solution.

In this part of your story you have 'caged birds' not 'nodding dogs'! This is because as you were going through your analysis of the consequences you would have had many facts and ideas that you rejected at that point for various reasons.

It is very important that you now refer to these rejected ideas at this stage of your story – because it deals effectively with all manner of things that may or may not be in your audience's mind. These ideas are 'trapped birds ready to fly frantically around the room' of your audience. Keep these 'birds' in their 'cages' and you do this by dealing with non-starter ideas and rejected ideas.

For example, John in the Family Grocers Division case study would see the 'cash and carry' warehouses as a bird and he would handle that now.

The **seventh** and **eighth** slides deal with the pivotal question and the answer in succession. Do you recall my story about you arriving at the '98th minute' as a 'hero' with the solution to the problem? Well, you are now at the 97th minute! If you have done your job well so far, your audience have just about bought into your presentation of the problem. The seventh and eight slides make you the 'hero'! All of your hard work so far in your analysis and synthesis is concentrated into these two slides – they are the core of your powerful story.

More important, they are the embodiment of the concept I mentioned in chapter 1 – the synergy between '**idea – plan – persuasion**'. You may recall that this is the relationship that natural leaders know the power of, and it is this powerful relationship that is at the core of the SCQuARE idea and process. And the core of your story.

> **Pivotal Question**
> How can . . . overcome . . .
> and/or exploit . . . to meet
> . . . to achieve . . .

> **Answer**
> Benefit
> Strategies

The pivotal question summarises into a single question the whole of the analysis of setting and consequences. If your audience buys into your pivotal question, then they will buy into your answer. Why? You will recall that the pivotal question contains the main action that will lead to your aim, this being the main benefit of your efforts. It is this main action that then expands into the answer and then, later, into your working plan. Buying into the question is, de facto, buying into the plan that achieves the aim that brings the benefits. Now you are the leader at the 99th minute. Your audience is now 'hooked' (as you promised in the opening slide) and the only issue you now have to deal with is how to make the whole plan work.

My final point is a simple practical one. The pivotal question and its answer can be lengthy and wordy (recall John's '**Qu**' and '**A**'). In written mode this is fine but in presentation mode you may wish to condense it.

The **ninth, tenth** and **eleventh** slides are your action plan and the plan summary – the '**RE**' of the SCQuARE mnemonic. There are three important points about these slides. First, potentially these slides could be highly detailed, thus making them dense in information, and very comprehensive in coverage, thus making them too many in number. This is a difficult issue to manage because it depends so much on your story and your audience. Try very hard to simplify and condense your plan at this stage of the presentation – you can always have backup

RE R	How
E	Why

charts and/or handouts or other secondary presentation aids.

Secondly, remember to present your information on the slides inductively – 'how' before 'why' or 'recommendation' before 'evidence'. You will recall from my earlier explanation of 'conclusion' before 'data' that this avoids the problem of your audience jumping to conclusions and/or becoming frustrated.

Here, you have to avoid 'cockroaches'. In the last chapter I mentioned the idea of pre-emptive questions (see page 108). These questions were potentially difficult questions that could be asked and for which you must have an answer. What I was doing at that point in the book was trying to get you to consider these questions very early – not in your story.

Finally, you must make sure everything fits, you cannot propose a solution to a problem you have never previously mentioned, or use a resource that you have not identified as a potential opportunity. You cannot pull the rabbit out of the conjurer's hat! If your audience says 'why are you proposing that?' or 'that is a surprise, when did that opportunity arise?' you have either 'not sold the problem' or you have positioned the opportunities inadequately, and therefore you have rabbits in your plan.

The **twelfth** slide is the final '**RE**' slide and it has a special role. Its first job is to summarise succinctly the presentation you have made. More important, it restates the main benefit of the proposals, which are normally the benefits of achieving the aim. If you have had lots of 'nodding dogs' in the presentation of your story then this benefit deserves a YES from your audience. Be confident, ask for the YES – you can even try the alternative close, 'Should I start this week or next week?'

Summary

The SCQuARE mnemonic starts with an aim and ends in a plan. The whole of SCQuARE tells a story and if this story is persuasive then you have the essential synergy that is the core of the SCQuARE process – **'idea – plan – persuasion'** – the essence of leadership and innovation.

The foundation of the story is a storyboard of about twelve 'building blocks', although this may be more or less depending upon your story. Each 'building block' has a headline and no more than three points that support the headline. This storyboard follows the SCQuARE process.

> **HEADLINE**
>
> Summary
>
> The benefit that deserves RE
>
> a YES
>
> Asking for a YES

Right at the start you state very clearly the aim and the benefit that this aim will bring. Then you build the 'problem' through the setting and the consequences – you can't sell the solution until you have sold the problem!

The core of your story is the pivotal question and the answer. Sell the pivotal question, containing a main action, and you sell your answer, de facto, your plan leading to the aim and its benefits.

If I had to summarise the whole of the SCQuARE process and the reason for its success with our clients then it would not be about a systematic thinking process or a planning process or any ideas like these, as worthwhile as they are. It would be that SCQuARE guides you to ask **'the right question'** and it is this question that, when answered, leads to your boss saying YES.

HOW CAN JOHN GET EVERYONE ON THE SAME PAGE?

The final part of the Family Grocers Division case study begins opposite.

In this final part of the case study I need to explain why I am taking a particular approach. Throughout the case study I have built up all of the issues in detail and I need to keep a lot of this detail in my explanations to satisfy the objective of the book being clear and useful to the reader – even though it means that I am putting a little too much information into the story slides that follow. Bear this in mind as you follow John's storyboard.

John's first task is to create the structure of the storyboard by creating headlines for the various parts of the SCQuARE process. John contains his story in the recommended twelve slides but his story is best told by emphasising the plan – or the '**RE**' of the SCQuARE mnemonic.

Once John is happy with his headline sequence, he builds up his story by bringing forward information from his previous workings. At this point John will be condensing and re-phrasing his information to suit the requirements of the presentation and his audience. At all times he will be putting the story into an imaginary conversation to make certain that the story is natural and succinct and as powerful as possible. Where necessary, John changes his headlines as he details his story.

Story headlines

Our agenda; to be the innovator in our industry   (S)

Objectives; to be the profitable number one   (S)

FGD is the group's star performer   (S)

Ceasing direct deliveries will be challenging   (C)

Asking the pivotal question   (Qu)

The best answer is the simplest   (A)

A rolling three-year contract is the key   (RE)

Focused incentives will build the volumes   (RE)

Focused promotions will create high motivation   (RE)

Being positive to cope with Walkers   (RE)

We have the resources to do the job   (RE)

And we have the commitment to achieve   (RE)

We have to be the innovator in our industry

Agenda

- business and market review
- the distribution challenge the division faces
- creating a new distribution solution
- a recommendation to transform the efficiency of our distribution and ensure we hit all our goals

We have the opportunity to create an unassailable lead in our industry

- whilst saving the costs we are seeking, we can achieve all our business objectives and continue to be the brand leader in all our segments

Continuing to be the profitable number one

The scope of these proposals

- focus the FGD division over the next three years

The aim of these proposals

- to continue to be the brand leader in all market segments

Our division objectives for next year are

- annual volume to grow by 8% to 6.5 m cases
- profit before tax to grow by 10% to £22 m
- at least £15 m in cost savings

FGD is the group's star performer

We lead a large mature market

- the total market is worth £500 m
- we are number one with 25% or £125 m sales; our nearest competitor, Walkers, has 15%

Nationwide availability is the key to our success

- there are 31,250 shops nationwide, 90% independently owned
- we currently service 22,000 by direct deliveries
- we have wide availability at 80% distribution

The division is critical to the group's success

- last year's sales were £125 m on 6.2 m cases, a growth of 8%
- 30% of all group volumes are derived from the division
- profits grew to £20 m, compared with flat profits across the group
- market share grew to 25%, compared with 18% across the group

Ceasing direct deliveries will be challenging

Ceasing direct deliveries is a manageable risk

- ceasing direct deliveries will save £15 m over three years
- but our success is built on nationwide availability so we need to change
- but still secure at least 80% coverage

No single channel offers the coverage we need

- no single alternative channel gives the coverage or terms we need
- we will need to combine the best channels to suit our needs
- Patel wholesalers and Rhonda merchandisers will give 80% coverage and in-store control

Expect a negative campaign from Walkers

- Walkers have confirmed their contracts for direct deliveries
- they will see our innovation and seek to steal our market share
- they will mount a campaign saying we are deserting the independents

We must steal share to meet our objectives

- market is forecast to grow at 2% versus our 5% objective

Asking the pivotal question

How can we combine the strengths of the alternative distribution options to retain our 80% market coverage and current in-store control, counter the threat of negative PR whilst exploiting our cost savings, ensuring that we meet our pre-set objectives and achieve our aim to continue to be the brand leader in all market segments?

The best answer is the simplest

We can meet our pre-set objectives and our aim if we retain our 80% market coverage by combining the coverage of Patel and Rhonda and reinvest some of the savings to provide focused distributor promotional support and counter the threat of Walkers' negative advertising.

A rolling three-year contract is the key

How we can succeed

- sign a three-year rolling contract with Patel and Rhonda that guarantees our minimum volumes and commits Patel and Rhonda to non-competitive trading

Why they will do this

- it gives virtually exclusive volumes from the market leader
- this stabilises their sales and market position at a high level

Focused incentives will build the volumes

How we can make money with our partners

- reduce the standard sales margin below a set limit
- introduce a high-value volume discount scheme for sales above the set limit and set clear targets for these higher volume sales

Why our partners will accept this

- changing the margin structure provides the financial opportunity for our partners to significantly boost their sales and earn higher profits from their efforts and this is only to our benefit

Focused promotions will create high motivation

How we can get motivation at the point-of-sale
- introduce a fully funded trade promotional campaign for our partners
- introduce a high-value sales force incentive scheme designed to reward results

Why our partners will accept this
- our promotions and incentives schemes will create the right motivation at the point-of-sale and this will reward our partners' efforts and loyalty

Being positive to cope with Walkers

How we can effectively counter their reactions
- introduce a trade advertising campaign designed to counter any negative advertising and PR from Walkers and any other competitor

Why we should do this
- it is essential that we counter any claims that Walkers make to the trade whilst at the same time strongly supporting the decision by Patel and Rhonda to partner us in our innovative strategy

We have the resources to do the job

How much it will cost

- starting in our new financial year, the high-value discount scheme will break even but we will provide £1m over three years for extra incentives and we will provide an additional £1m over three years for all promotional support and specific campaigns. A total cost of £2m over three years under-written from savings

Why this is excellent value

- for the next three years our forecasts are:

  volumes at 7m, 8m and 9.5m cases

  market share at 26%, 27% and 28%

  profits at £22m, £25m and £28m

And we have the commitment to achieve

Summary

- we fully support the decision to cease direct deliveries but to continue to be the market leader and achieve our business objectives we need to innovate
- we need to combine the best distributors into a new three-year strategy and effectively support this decision with focused promotions and incentives

We have the opportunity to lead from the front

- whilst saving the costs we are seeking, we can achieve all our business objectives and continue to be the brand leader in all our segments

We believe that our strategy is good and robust

Should we get on with the job?

YOUR PROJECT

Your story headlines

Your headline

Point 1

- short descriptive text
- short descriptive text
- short descriptive text

Point 2

- short descriptive text
- short descriptive text
- short descriptive text

Point 3

- short descriptive text
- short descriptive text
- short descriptive text

Your headline

Your text for the Pivotal Question and Answer

practise

'Great! Green lights all the way
...just like being at work!'

CHAPTER 8

THE ONE-CHANCE PITCH

Now that you are at the end of this book I thought I would provide you with another chance to practise your new skills.

The case study below is a very interesting situation that needs resolution – you have to make a very strong but short presentation to Jim Albright, an impatient Vice President who does not suffer fools.

Case study – one-chance pitch

You are the Director of Sales and Marketing of Mogul Mobile Communications Limited (MMC), a subsidiary of Mogul Mobiles International (MMI). Despite tough economic times, MMC has been very successful over the last year – increasing market share to 53%, volume up 12% and making a net profit at $90 m, 9% over budget on sales of $804 m. It was your first year as Director, and with inflation running at 6%, you had delivered a very impressive performance, a credit to you and your team.

However, this year things have changed. Cherry Phones International Inc. (Cherry), MMC's biggest international rival, has entered the market, buying out a local telecommunications company called Happy Phones (Happy) with the declared aim of doubling Happy's market share.

At the time, MMC executives had poured scorn on this possibility, but three months into the New Year you are now looking at some very sorry figures. In the euphoria of last year's success, you had allowed yourself to go for a very aggressive budget with sales targets up 15% to $925 m. Now, the results for the first quarter have made you feel quite ill: at this rate they wouldn't be 15% up on last year but 10% down!

The issues were very clear: Cherry's new initiatives and MMI's anti-inflation policy. Mogul Mobiles International was badly hit with the recession in the Far East. Anxious to maintain profits and ride out the recession without losing key staff, they made the policy decision to hold down staff costs worldwide by limiting annual salary increases to inflation.

Cherry had no such restraints. Everyone agreed that MMC had one of the best sales and marketing teams and Cherry were brazenly trying to recruit key MMC staff with salaries inflated 20–30%. MMC had already lost three key account managers, the sales manager and five field sales staff. You knew that at least six others were being courted, and you had strong reasons for thinking that confidential marketing information was being leaked to your competitor.

You explained this situation to Fred Allego the MD of MMC, and asked him to approach HQ in Brussels to make your company an exception. Fred had firmly declined, *'I am not going to be the first to break the Board's policy decision. No way! You had better think up something new.'*

You met your team and came up with ideas for non-salary benefits that would encourage people to stay and enable recruitment. You have made a possible list and had it approved in principle by the head of HR and Fred Allego. Both thought it had promise.

Fred's response was typical: *'Yeah, it might work, but you'll have to sell it to the Area Vice President. He'll be here for a half-day stopover, next week, on his way to Brussels. I can get you twenty minutes with him.'*

You are stunned. Fred knew that Jim 'One Chance' Albright, the Vice President in Brussels, was a notoriously tough man to persuade.

You are to prepare a presentation to Jim Albright persuading him to agree to your ideas for non-salary benefits for the sales and marketing team. You might find the additional notes on the following page useful.

Character information on Jim Albright:

He is a workaholic

He is fiercely loyal to Mogul and a dedicated one-company man

Does not suffer fools and demands clear factual communication

Can be notoriously aggressive and impatient at repetition and waffle

His reputation was for one chance only, hence his nickname

The sales and marketing team is made up as follows:

Director of Sales and Marketing – YOU

Sales Manager (now vacant)

One Marketing Manager and three Brand Managers

Six Key Account Managers (three slots now vacant)

Media Manager and her Assistant

24 Field Sales (five vacant)

Current salaries and perks were:

Salaries in the mid-upper quartile

Annual profit bonus

Two weeks' annual holiday rising to three weeks after 10 years

A contributory pension scheme

Staff canteen

SETTING

DEFINE THE ENTITY

What is the subject?

What is the scope?

What is the time frame?

Is the project within your decision
accountabilities?

DEFINE THE AIM

What is the end point?

What are the measures or definitions of
success of this end point?

What is the time frame of this end point?

ARE THERE ANY PRE-SET
OBJECTIVES?

(If there are no pre-set objectives then don't
invent any!)

CREATE THE SETTING

What are the main relevant and important
facts that underpin the setting for your project?

What are the positive factors that will lead to
your aim or that you want to build on?

POSITIVE 'SO WHAT?'

Interpret the main groups of facts in the most
positive way to give more powerful meaning.

Ask 'so what?' of all the groups of facts.

CONSEQUENCES

WHAT HAS CHANGED?

Use this checklist:

Has this factor changed?
What created this change?
When did this change occur?
Is this a positive or negative change?
What are the consequences of this change?
Can I cope with these consequences?
Has this change exposed a major risk?
What happens if this factor has not changed?
What are the consequences of lack of change?
Can I cope with these consequences?
Has this lack of change exposed a major risk?
Should I take into account any new factors?

WHAT COULD CHANGE?

Use this checklist:

Could this factor change?
If so, what would create this change?
When would this change occur?
Is this a positive or negative change?
What are the consequences of this change?
Could I cope with these consequences?
Does this change expose a major risk?
What happens if this factor does not change?
What are the consequences of lack of change?
Could I cope with these consequences?
Does this lack of change expose a major risk?
Should I take into account any new factors?

ANY COMPLICATIONS?

Use this checklist:

Could this factor complicate my plans?
If so, what are the negative consequences?
Could I cope with these consequences?
Does this complication expose a major risk?
What happens if I resolve this complication?
Will the resolution expose more consequences?
Could I cope with these new consequences?
What are the limiting factors?
Do these limiting factors have a consequence?
Could I cope with these limiting factors?
Should I take into account any new factors?

Don't forget to group your factors

153

Now create your causal chain diagram using the template below.

Causal Chain template

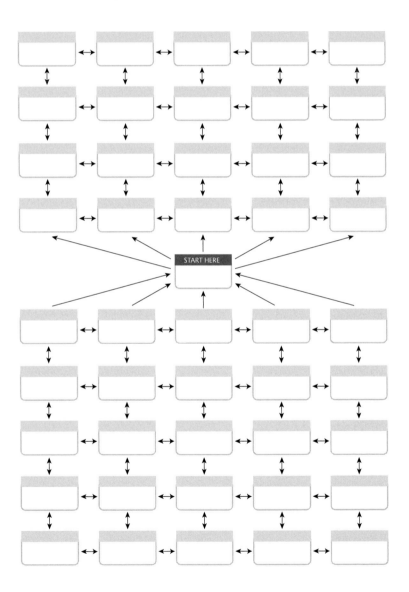

PIVOTAL QUESTION

From your setting bring forward your entity, aim and any pre-set objectives.

Refer back to your causal chain diagram and clarify your main action.

Review all your factors in your project and identify the main negative factors that will impede your progress towards your aim and that must be overcome.

Review all your factors in your project and identify the main positive factors that you can exploit in order to progress towards your aim

Use the template overleaf and build (from the bottom up) your first attempt at your pivotal question.

Pivotal Question template

Qu

How can   [I/We/The Entity]

[Main action]
....

in order to Overcome: and Exploit:

[Issue]   [Opportunity]
....

[Issue]   [Opportunity]
....

[Issue]   [Opportunity]
....

[Issue]   [Opportunity]
....

[Issue]   [Opportunity]
....

To achieve   [Pre-set objectives]
....

And/or   [Aim]
....

ANSWER

From your experience and using any creativity techniques, create a long list of individual strategies that could lead to the achievement of your aim.

Shortlist your strategies into an overall strategy.

Is your overall strategy:

    Compelling and believable?

    Does it have clear benefits?

    Does it state 'what'?

    Is it clear and succinct?

Insert your overall combined strategies into the strategy matrix below, and evaluate.

Strategy Matrix template

The Entity				
Aim				
Pre-set Objectives				
Main Action				
Changes/Complications				
Unexploited opportunities				
Strategies for evaluation				

Qu Your Pivotal Question was:

A Your Answer is (subject to revision by later action plans):

RECOMMENDATIONS AND EVIDENCE

Bring your answer forward and keep it uppermost in your workings.

Develop your main ideas and support ideas here:

Consider your pre-emptive questions.
Use this checklist:

Are your strategies clear and succinct?

Are your objectives well defined and clear?

Are your priorities well defined and clear?

Have you considered all the critical matters?

What are the risks if problems arise?

Have you identified all important matters?

Have you identified all important constraints?

Could a constraint become a limiting factor?

Could a constraint become a down-size risk?

Do you have adequate resources for the job?

Are your financial expectations realistic?

Will you meet investment and cash objectives?

Do you have the right team and skills?

Is your team committed to the objectives?

Have you considered all important stakeholders?

Do you have a communication plan?

What are your plans for managing change?

What are your plans for involving all affected?

What problems can you foresee at this stage?

Are there matters ahead that are highly critical?

What contingency plans have you considered?

Recommendations & Evidence template

SUMMARISED ANSWER	Develop new channels supported with focused promotions

Main idea	
HOW	WHY

Support Ideas

HOW 1	WHY 1
HOW 2	WHY 2

HOW 3	WHY 3
HOW 4	WHY 4

HOW 5	WHY 5

Resource context	
Finance	WHY

Timings	WHY
Responsibility	WHY

Your story headlines

Your headline

Point 1

- short descriptive text
- short descriptive text
- short descriptive text

Point 2

- short descriptive text
- short descriptive text
- short descriptive text

Point 3

- short descriptive text
- short descriptive text
- short descriptive text

Your headline

Your text for the Pivotal Question and Answer

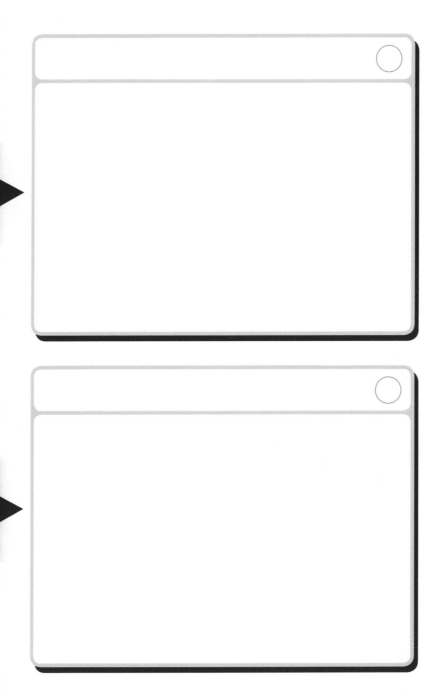

BREAKER

At the end of chapter five, 'Finding the Right Answer', I made a note that the right answer has come about by you using your innate critical and analytical capabilities. These capabilities are located in the 'left hand' side of your brain. I mentioned that if you wish you can continue to use these same capabilities in chapter six, 'Making the Answer Work'.

However, I also mentioned that there was another way – a way that is highly creative. This means that 'Making your Answer Work' could be a more imaginative set of ideas that could lead to higher innovation. This way uses more of the 'right hand' side of your brain – the side that is creative and imaginative.

The goal is to use both sides of the brain in harmony. I call this **whole brain thinking** and this is what this chapter is about. This means we can enhance SCQuARE and make it even more powerful – put together we get Whole Brain Strategy.

Our name for this significant enhancement is BREAKER, which simply means that we BREAK our normal way of thinking from the critical and analytical to the creative and imaginative. We call these new ideas **Big Ideas Realised**, the title of the next chapter.

These same ideas are also the basis of a training course called BREAKER that is now being used by our clients either as part of our SCQUARE services or as a stand-alone service.

There are many people involved in the BREAKER service. The people who were instrumental in its development and commercialisation are acknowledged below. But there are others. There are the client consultants and there are those who support with administration and materials. All of these people are dedicated to making BREAKER a world class service.

In effect we are a close team and this needs to be acknowledged. So, even though I write in the first person, the 'I', this must not detract from the team efforts and the high levels of collaboration with creativity specialists that makes the BREAKER service such a success. I sincerely thank all of those who work on BREAKER.

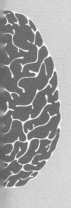

ACKNOWLEDGEMENTS

There are many who have contributed their time and skills to making BREAKER a success. Each had a passion for the ideas and each had a dedication to making it work. I would like to thank John Wright, ex-MD of Saatchi and Saatchi, Andrew Wilkie, ex-MD of Saatchi and Saatchi, GUM division, Martin Cleator and Paul Wilkinson. They were a formidable team and the creative drive and inspiration behind the development of BREAKER and its commercial success.

BRE∧KER

It was 'dress as a potato' day again in the Imagination Department.

Creativity comes from looking for the unexpected and
stepping outside your own experience

Masaru Ibuka

CHAPTER 9

BIG IDEAS REALISED

Above all human traits, imagination is the one that inspires us the most. It makes us dream, it makes us feel complete and it leads us to achieve our greatest goals. Without imagination, our lives would be empty.

And imagination is one of the greatest corporate assets. Bill Gates of Microsoft says that his leading company, *'is a company that manages imagination'*. The same could be said of Apple, Virgin and all the other companies, large and small, that endeavour to lead the way.

Whether it is our own lives, our businesses, our arts, our science, our technology and our cultures as a whole, imagination is at the front of all our endeavours. Imagination is best described by Albert Einstein, *'Imagination is more important than knowledge. For while knowledge defines all we currently know and understand, imagination points to all we might yet discover and create.'*

The origins of BREAKER

BREAKER is our concept of structured imagination. It was designed to meet a real business need and it grew out of necessity. Why is this the case? Around 2008, during the financial shocks that hit the world, most western developed economies were in deep recession. Most corporate reactions were typical – risk averse leadership, cost cutting and business restructuring. And quite rightly so.

At this same time, my company was as busy as ever as our clients realised that the same old ways of working were not good enough. The universal managerial questions were, 'how do we innovate to avoid discounting ourselves out of business in the current climate?', 'how can we compete better to stand out?', 'what do we need to do to differentiate ourselves?' These were the right questions but the answers that rose to the top were not inspiring. Good answers, but probably just the same as any of their competitors. It was clear, the answers were not innovative, not brave, and not creative and above all else, they were not imaginative.

This was the need we saw – an almost universal corporate need for developing more inspiring and brave answers. We could meet this real need if we had a concept that would enhance our idea generation within our SCQuARE process. Importantly, the concept had to work really well independently and bring benefits as a stand-alone working tool.

I put together a team of our consultants and alumni. The team had the creative drive of the imaginative people of Saatchi and Saatchi and the strategic and the logical practicality of McKinsey. Their brief was to devise a concept for developing imaginative and creative ideas that could transform the ideas, potentials and activities of our clients.

At the core of their concept was the idea that imaginative, brave and innovative ideas would only come from 'breaking' previous patterns of thinking. These established patterns of thinking are excellent if you want to evolve a product or service – make it better than it is now. But, they are not the ways of thinking for

170

coming up with the radical ideas that inspire and create leadership. How to 'BREAK' these traditional patterns of thinking is the foundation of our BREAKER service.

SCQuARE and BREAKER together

What was the inspiration behind BREAKER and how does BREAKER integrate with the SCQuARE process?

My story starts in San Francisco. I was leading a crucial strategic workshop on SCQuARE with one of our clients, a major international telecommunications company. It was very enjoyable with lots of hard work, excitement and humorous banter. As always with this client the participants were very bright and thoughtful.

I had reached the stage of summarising the importance of the 'pivotal question', a concept that you are now familiar with from chapter 4 of this book.

I stressed that to get the right answers you had to work very hard at defining the pivotal question. You did this by making sure that you had alignment on the setting and consequences and this helped you to get alignment on the pivotal question. Humorously, I reinforced my words with the idea that getting alignment on the pivotal question was like reaching the summit of a mountain.

'Once you get there', I said, 'you can proudly put your flag in and take a deep satisfying breath'; the participants knowingly smiled and acknowledged the point.

Apart from Bob! He was a very quietly spoken participant from Alberta, the ski capital of Canada. Although very much involved, he was a reflective learner and had said very little, until now. He had a challenging idea:

'Ross,' he queried, 'whether you are mountain climber or skier, there is one simple truth about a mountain – most accidents happen on the way down!'

In his insightful way he was saying that it's fine to define the problem but in his experience most matters that create trouble are matters you encounter during implementation. That important comment stuck with me, because it is true.

As I flew back from San Francisco that weekend, Bob's query played on my mind. I thought of all the times in my own career when I had 'proudly put my flag in' as a well thought out strategy was accepted. Only to find later as the implementation started that the plan ran into trouble. And I thought of all the times that our clients' strategies ran into some trouble because their solutions lacked creativity and imagination – same old, same old!

The more I reflected upon Bob's query the more I saw the truth. 'Most accidents happen on the way down' or strategies run into trouble because we try to 'come down the mountain the same way we went up' or 'we use the same way of thinking about a solution as we use to think about a problem'. This is why I set up the task team to find an exciting way of going forward – a way that we named BREAKER.

So, how do SCQuARE and BREAKER fit together? Now that you have read this book you will recall that SCQuARE is a mnemonic as shown in the diagram. The '**S**' the setting, '**C**' the consequences and '**Qu**' the pivotal question are critical and analytical processes dependent upon our logical thoughts and reflections. Then we begin to change the way we think so that '**A**' the answer and '**RE**' the action plan (recommendations and evidence) are imaginative and inspiring and dependent upon our creative thoughts and reflections.

You can see where BREAKER adds value. Depending upon the type of '**A**', we have, BREAKER becomes the best tool to realise big ideas. When it is clear that the '**A**' requires radical solutions and/or highly imaginative innovations then BREAKER is the perfect tool to use. When '**A**' requires less radical solutions then BREAKER has less added value because less powerful creative tools are adequate.

So, BREAKER is a very powerful enhancement to SCQuARE for use in those highly important strategic situations where a solution has to lead to a wholly new direction. If you want to lead in the future then BREAKER is used – it answers the CEO's plea '*Where are the inspiring solutions that will make us number one?*'

I firmly believe that we need to do things differently. If you get to the top of a very high and important 'mountain', yes put in your 'flag' but DO NOT come down the same way! Or, 'do not use the same way of thinking about a solution as you use to think about a problem'.

I like to refer to BREAKER and SCQuARE together as 'whole brain thinking' because it combines the left and right brains together in a powerful tool, as the diagram here shows:

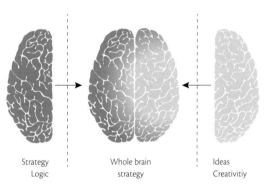

| Strategy | Whole brain | Ideas |
| Logic | strategy | Creativitiy |

Finally, Bob is now happier. Yes, 'most accidents do happen on the way down from the mountain top' but for the radical, imaginative, brave and inspiring solutions then BREAKER is the way down!

A word about barriers

BREAKER has a number of distinct stages and I will go through these in a moment. But before this, I would like to lower three barriers that might reside deep in your

psyche about imagination and creativity. These deep barriers are very important to you because they limit your capability to use BREAKER to its full power.

It is interesting to note that these three important barriers come from our history. Bertram Russell's book *History of Western Philosophy*, covers the whole of our heritage from the Pre-Socratics to the Philosophy of Logical Analysis – a history covering 585 BC to the present day. Over these 2600 years of western thought one collected set of ideas have had the most impact on how we think. These are the ideas of Socrates, Plato and Aristotle.

Socrates (469 BC – 399 BC) is credited as one of the founders of western philosophy. We know about him from the dialogues of Plato, his protégé and student. He is best known for his work on ethics but he also lends his name to the Socratic Method – a way of teaching in which questions are asked to find answers and create fundamental insight. His pedagogy was what we would now refer to as creating hypotheses to prove or disprove.

Plato (424 BC – 348 BC) was a mathematician and writer of 36 philosophic dialogues covering logic, ethics, rhetoric and mathematics. In particular he is credited with Platonic Realism, a fascinated search for intellectual truth that was more perfect than physical truth.

'The only way is ethics'

Aristotle (384 BC – 322 BC) was a student of Plato. Aristotle was a polymath so his works covered physics, metaphysics, ethics, poetry, government and rhetoric amongst others. But, it was his acclaimed views on the physical sciences that shaped medieval scholarship and the later Renaissance. In particular, it was his work on formal logic using the so-called scientific method that shaped the thinking of the western world.

All three philosophers, I smilingly refer to them as 'the Greek gang of three', have conditioned the way we think. We have been trained over centuries of education and cultural conditioning to be highly logical, critical and systematic. As important as these are, you and I have not had the same degree of historical attention paid to our imagination and creativity. We have not been trained and educated in using our whole brain, our critical capabilities and our creative capabilities as one.

Mr Edison often felt he was on the brink of a great idea.

It is this marvellous heritage that has rooted, deep in our psyches, the three barriers to your creativity. The first common barrier is the idea that **every problem has only one solution or answer.** It's easy to see how this comes about. You work hard trying to find a solution. Then, a solution comes and you accept it. Job done! This is not the case.

You may recall the very popular quotation *'Genius is one percent inspiration and ninety-nine percent perspiration'.* This saying is from Thomas Edison, the inventor of the light bulb. Of course, nowadays, we are blasé about this invention but in 1880 when Edison patented the 'long lasting filament' it was an idea about to change the course of the history of the world and light the course of industry. What is less well known about Edison's work on the filament is that he tried well over a thousand different types of filaments before he found his final solution. When asked about his frustration on his journey he replied, *'I've gained a lot of knowledge, I now know a thousand things that don't work'.* That is ninety nine percent perspiration!

Now I'm not suggesting that you try a thousand solutions before you settle on one. Just pay heed to the barrier that exists that every problem has only one solution or answer. This is simply not the case.

The second very common barrier is the belief that **it cannot be done** in my Company. This amounts to giving up even before you start. Of course, history is littered with proof that it can be done. Yes, man can fly in planes, rockets do leave the earth's atmosphere, and I can speak with somebody thousands of miles away and so on. Really, it cannot be done should be replaced by it hasn't been done yet, I'll do it!

Truly, it only takes imagination and you have that in abundance. Without doubt, you have to educate yourself back into creativity. Then, like a child, you have to be willing to release its power.

But, most times you don't and you have inside you a third barrier that

'Of course I can do it, I don't know why you have to be so "Anti" everything'

shouts **I cannot do it.** You might think that you are not creative – *'I'm good at getting things done but I'm useless at coming up with bright ideas'* you say. Sometimes you think that people might laugh at your ideas. Sometimes you think that all ideas will be rejected because you are new to a team. Sometimes you don't talk about a really 'off-the-wall' idea because you know the team likes ideas that conform to the team culture. And, the situations go on and on. But, let me make it clear – we are all creative, we just need to find it and use it.

This is one of the reasons why BREAKER is such a success. It gives you permission and it gives you the tools to be outlandish and foolish and brave. And, BREAKER says **it hasn't been done yet but we are going to do it**.

Not only this, BREAKER reminds you that you are curious, that you do enjoy difficult challenges, that you are optimistic, that you like to dream, that you like to really challenge long-held assumptions and finally, that you do like to work hard and persevere.

Robert Frost, an American poet, in a sentence described our potential weakness:

'The brain is a wonderful organ; it starts the moment you get up in the morning and does not stop until you get to the office.'

'Monday to Friday, I'm paid to think inside the box.'

See, we can be our own worst enemy! Heed the barriers but work to overcome them. BREAKER will show you how.

How BREAKER works

Let me now describe BREAKER and how it works for you. There are five stages to follow; **focus, chunking, generating, landing and activating**. I refer to these as a creative journey and they are designed to uncover the transformational idea – the idea that is inspiring.

On the diagram below, BREAKER recognises both the left and right sides of the brain. You can see the top half, the critical capability and you can see the bottom half, the very important creative capability. These are working in harmony but their emphasis in use changes as you progress through the creative journey.

The **focus** is about identifying the subject. This may be a strategic requirement or the answer that has to be developed. Identifying the subject is not necessarily

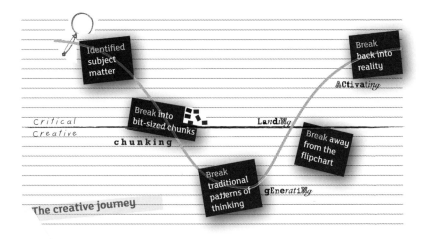

easy. As Albert Einstein says *'the mere formulation of a problem is far more essential than its solution'*. Clearly, it goes without saying that if you do not define the subject well then you do not have the focus as you go through the BREAKER creative journey.

That is why the SCQuARE process is so good – **'Qu'** the pivotal question would have directed you to the right **'A'** the answer. In turn, the answer matrix creates foci or the identified subjects for BREAKER.

You can't be creative with a requirement that is too big. Therefore **chunking** is the next stage after identifying the subject. It is about breaking the subject down into separate parts or known categories. They are bite size chunks that help us see a clearer picture.

For example, how do you deal with a requirement like 'internal communications'? This is a huge requirement so we have to chunk it like in the diagram:

Here you see 'internal communications' has been **'chunked up'** to show corporate communications. Also, it has been **'chunked across'** to show consumer

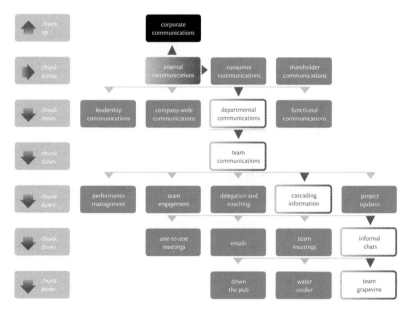

communications and shareholder communications. Then, at different levels, shown in the white boxes, it has been **'chunked down'** to show: departmental communications; team communications; information; informal chats and team grapevine.

It is always a good idea to name your chunks with an emotive idea and/or benefit, for example, 'team grapevine' could be 'I heard it on the Grapevine . . .' Giving a chunk a fun or more memorable name allows you to move away from the rational into the creative, it acts as a springboard. We often end up with song titles or TV Shows, which automatically changes the energy in the room.

The next stage is **generating**. You will recall from the creative journey diagram that generating is a wholly creative process. It is all about really good ideas – the more the better.

There are four good techniques to BREAK traditional patterns of thinking. I use one, two or more of the four techniques on the categories I have chunked up and/or chunked across and/or chunked down. As you can imagine you now have a very rich working palette for creating and bouncing ideas around.

The first idea generating technique is to **play with words** using idea associations. This is a very simple and effective concept. You start with any part of your chunking (say) 'team grapevine'. What ideas, phrases or words are associated with team grapevine?

First, let me give my chunk an emotional benefit – I want my team grapevine to buzz with great team information. It's a great buzz.

Now, what do I associate with a great buzz? Bees searching for nectar and bees returning to the hive with nectar and a message about where the nectar is from. And now, a happy swarm, moving in the same direction.

What do I associate with 'a happy swarm?' Smiles and laughter; milling about; playful games. Now, what do I associate with 'the same direction?' Guidance; maps; orienteering; destination.

As you can see, a germ of a good idea is emerging – a playful team game using grapevine messages as clues to a new team policy.

The next concept is to **play with the facts** using the 'amplify' technique. This technique takes a subject, let's use 'team grapevine' again, and then applies a number of ideas that question the facts as we know them. For example, the team grapevine is for unimportant and informal information.

But, what happens if I **adapt** it so it handles important and formal information. Or, I **modify** it so that it forms part of team briefings. Or, I **put to another use** like generating improvement ideas and suggestions. Or, I **lose the issue** – a virtual 'water cooler' on the intranet. You can see the technique is stretching me in new directions and all sorts of ideas can come out.

'Yes, hi Jean, I can hear you, this is great, the new communications tool is already bearing fruit!'

You can play with the facts in different ways by creating a new paradigm. I call this 'constructive disruption'. This is very powerful. The idea is to 'disrupt' your thinking by turning it on its head. It is very simple to do. You take a key principle or fact about your chunk and then create a statement that challenges it or contradicts it. You can be as openly disruptive and provocative as you wish.

For example, in our internal communications case I could say 'internal communication is a waste of leadership time'. The task now is to list out what is negative, what is positive and what is interesting. Negative could be 'drastic deterioration in staff morale' or 'lack of alignment on key policies'. Positive could be 'leadership time freed up for priority tasks' or 'increase in team initiative taking'. Interesting could be 'How do staff access important information?' or 'How do staff get feedback and assess their own performance?'

Here you see that I now have a whole array of provocative ideas. I can play with these. For example, what internal communications system do I need to make sure that I align policies but gain the benefits of more leadership time? Or, would self-assessment of performance lead to much higher team morale?' And so on.

We can enhance constructive disruption by adding 'what if . . .?' questions. What if company directors joined our team grapevine? What if a team member received a financial reward for passing on important team information?

The next concept is to **play with the context** by looking where the problem has been solved elsewhere. For example, why do children like to communicate by playing games? How would a child look at my team grapevine? What improvements would they make?

Or you can play with the context by a visualisation to act it out and get into the problem. Why don't I follow an important piece of team information through the grapevine and see what happens? Let me draw a diagram of what I think will happen.

Finally, **play with the stimulus**. You can do this humorously and with dream-like meaning. Randomise what you see, hear and think. Do team members giggle at the water cooler? What happens if I put chairs at the water cooler? Select random images and then make associations until you find things that just make you grin and smile. Or, associate with nature. Do rabbits use a grapevine?

As you can see all of these four generating techniques are designed to stretch your mind and break out of just using critical thinking. Use all four techniques together or just use a couple or just one, as you see fit.

Yes, some of the ideas are silly. But, what is wrong with that? Yes, most can be impractical at first sight. But, with more work they could be most inspiring. Anyway, one thing I now know from these thoughts and musings, as BREAKER says with force, '**it hasn't been done yet but we are going to do it**.'

The next stage is **landing**. This symbolises breaking away from the flip chart and landing the idea. As we were deep into idea generating using the various techniques a lot of ideas would have been created. Some at first sight would be good, others would be bad. Some would be very simple and others would be complicated. Some of these ideas would have a life, a quality that shouts 'look at me more'.

Landing is about giving your ideas a visual life. They are not just headings or words on a flipchart. You are not eliminating good ideas at this stage, you are creating pictures and interesting details – like

'. . . not so much a "99" as a "999"!'

drawing a story. Let's imagine I have (say) five ideas about ice cream. Each idea needs further development but at this stage I just want to visualise the idea to a point where I can show it easily to others.

This is also the stage where ideas can take on more meaning. For example, in the diagram you can see the idea of a fizzy bomb. Nice idea – a black bomb shaped ice cream made even more fun and very exciting by making it tick if shaken. But, 'best not sold in airports'!

We now come to the final stage, **activating**. We are now firmly back in reality but we are still creative – we need to make good ideas work. Our job is to develop any good ideas further and then select the best. Don't forget, if BREAKER has done its job well then amongst the candidate ideas is an idea that is brave and inspiring. We have to make this idea practical and commercial.

All businesses have their own commercial assessment procedures – generally a list of criteria that projects are evaluated against. We can use these basic ideas at this stage for selecting the best idea.

The most common is the weighted scoring systems. This is a list of selection criteria, which are weighted. For example, there may be five important selection criteria but they are not all equal in importance. Each criterion is given a weight, normally a weight out of a hundred points, and then each idea is assessed against these weighted criteria. Generally, the idea with the highest overall score is considered the best. But as we all know – we select the one we like!

But, at BREAKER we have our own criteria for any ideas coming out of the BREAKER process. We use our own brutal selection criteria.

We are at the end of the BREAKER creative journey – a journey that promises to use your critical AND creative capabilities in harmony. You started with an identified subject – a focus. You had fun breaking the subject down into chunks – up, down and across and naming them in non business language. You then played with words, played with the facts, played with the context and finally,

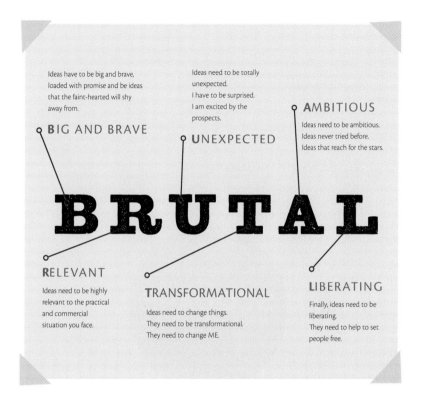

Ideas have to be big and brave, loaded with promise and be ideas that the faint-hearted will shy away from.

BIG AND BRAVE

Ideas need to be totally unexpected.
I have to be surprised.
I am excited by the prospects.

UNEXPECTED

AMBITIOUS

Ideas need to be ambitious.
Ideas never tried before.
Ideas that reach for the stars.

BRUTAL

RELEVANT

Ideas need to be highly relevant to the practical and commercial situation you face.

TRANSFORMATIONAL

Ideas need to change things.
They need to be transformational.
They need to change ME.

LIBERATING

Finally, ideas need to be liberating.
They need to help to set people free.

played with the stimulus. Out of this you had a lot of ideas. You drew pictures about the ideas and visualised these ideas to the point where you were then able to use criteria to help with the selection of the best idea ready for activation.

I started this chapter with the truthful and wise words of Albert Einstein reminding us that imagination points to all that we might yet discover and create. I finish this chapter with his words reminding us that life is a balance and all life is funny. He had a formula for success:

'If A is a success in life, then A equals x+y+z. Where x is work, y is play and z is keeping your mouth shut!'

Even the world's most renowned scientist was a child at heart. Reminding us to be always humble and always one step away from a wry smile.

Think • Plan • Deliver

CHAPTER 10

GLOBAL LEADERS IN STRATEGIC, CREATIVE & PERSUASIVE THINKING

SCQUARE International are world leaders in providing strategic, creative and storytelling techniques to build and sell the right plans. We do this via proprietary training and consultancy products, backed by interactive online support, unlocking elite skills otherwise reserved for specialists.

We have helped to drive the performance of hundreds of the world's leading businesses and tens of thousands of their people in 73 plus countries since 1993.

We work with business leaders to help them tackle big complex challenges – the kind that you know you have to address but no one knows quite how. Helping their teams to build and agree strategic plans, with unexpected but relevant creativity, at a pace and precision unimaginable through conventional working practices:

Consultancy and Training mix determined by client needs

We are able to offer a variety of service combinations to achieve the objectives and desired client outcomes.

We run monthly 2-day **Open Programmes** for SCQuARE training for delegates from different companies. This is an ideal trial opportunity to experience the process or for small teams.

Alternatively we run **Corporate programmes** with individual clients. Programmes run between 2–4 days depending on a pre-agreed agenda.

All programmes are highly engaging and participative, delivered through a blend of theory and hands-on small group work, applying techniques to fun but intense case studies.

Consultancy and Facilitation of live challenges, enabling real time return on Investment

Increasingly our work is about delivering game changing skills and then facilitating these new skills as they are applied to LIVE work challenges, harnessing all the relevant managers, empowering them to create and own their own plans.

SCQuARE Strategy Into Action marries the leadership vision with the management's knowledge, to create a workable plan that will deliver alignment, ownership and commitment in a time frame unimaginable through normal working practices, and at a fraction of the cost of traditional management consultants.

SCQuARE for Sales gives you the skill to get inside your customer's mind and convert your analysis and insight into a clear, winning sales pitch with your credentials pitched as the solution to the customer's problem, thereby reducing the inevitable negotiation costs.

InterACT is a natural accompaniment to SCQuARE. Once delegates have learnt to create a foolproof plan they may feel the need to improve the softer skills necessary to deliver the content with maximum impact, influence and confidence. Delivered by our specialist voice and performance coaches, InterACT is a blend of theory, individual analysis and feedback using case studies and/or live work.

BREAKER is a stand-alone toolkit for creativity and idea generation. BREAKER provides people with the skills and techniques to generate transformational ideas and turn them into memorable two-dimensional outputs.

SCQuARE and BREAKER is 'Whole Brain Strategy': a unique 3–4 day event that combines the analytical power of SCQuARE to find the right strategic direction and then applies BREAKER's disruptive thinking to generate unexpected but relevant ideas and develop the complete plan. It is the art and science of strategy formulation, created and owned by the team.

Ross left school at 16 years because the school and he were 'no longer on the same page' – they wanted to teach him chemistry and woodwork and he wanted to learn how to create and sell things and make money.

At 19 years he got a job as a trainee salesman with a division of Trebor Sharpes – a job he relished. He then secured positions with Polycell and Carnation developing his skills and experience in sales and marketing.

Later, a sales development management role in PepsiCo proved to be the single most important career move of his life. He spent nearly a decade with PepsiCo working in Europe, the Middle East and Africa, working his way up the organisation to hold a number of Vice President positions.

Not only did PepsiCo stretch him but it also provided the realisation that the difference between success and failure both as an individual or team and irrespective of geography or function was in having the ability to think strategically, to create and sell plans that commanded a decision. Yet astonishingly this crucial skill was not formally taught anywhere and only practiced by the elite management consultants. This was the inspiration to create his business SCQUARE International and write this book.

Ross is married with three children and lives in Surrey, England. He is a passionate supporter of Crystal Palace Football Club and a lover of golf.

Index

INDEX